CORPORATE PLANNING
AS A CREATIVE PROCESS

Action Laid Out In Advance

by

George C. Sawyer

Published by
Planning Executives Institute
5500 College Corner Pike
Oxford, Ohio 45056

658.401
S 371

First Printing, April 1983

ISBN 0-912841-00-1

Published by
        Planning Executives Institute
        5500 College Corner Pike
        Oxford, Ohio 45056

To Margo

ABOUT THE AUTHOR

Dr. Sawyer heads Management Technology & Resources, consultants in corporate strategy and business growth. He is also Professor, Management & Administration Program, Economics Department, City College of New York. Previously, he had served as Director of Corporate Planning & Development for Hoffmann-La Roche, moving from the Corporate Planning Department of American Cyanamid, where he had a successful earlier career in production and development management.

Dr. Sawyer holds BS and MS in Chemical Engineering from the University of Wisconsin, MBA and PhD in Management from New York University and is licensed as a Professional Engineer. He is a Senior Editor of **Planning Review,** and member of a number of professional societies including Planning Executives Institute. He has written many journal articles, including several for **Managerial Planning.** His books include **Business and Society,** Houghton Mifflin, 1979, **The Quiet Crisis of Public Pensions,** Aspen Institute, 1980, and he is currently writing a business policy text.

PREFACE

This book is about strategic planning. It is for those who wish to learn about, manage or work in the strategic planning area. It deals with the problems and opportunities of such planning, and the respective roles of line and staff.

As a book on planning it bridges from the work of individual managers to top management and integrates to the central strategy of the organization. The focus is (1) on a pattern of activity and an approach to the planning tasks in organizations that can aid in more effective management of that component of management activity, and (2) on the central issues and choices that can make the planning effort successful and rewarding.

From my own approaches to the challenges of planning, and my own appraisal of the needs and problems in presenting planning to groups who need to understand it, has come the present book. It is born out of experience in line and staff management positions with several corporations.

I believe that this book will be useful to members of the business community who wish to learn more about planning and strategy, and also as a text for the type of strategic planning course I have taught to MBA students. It is not intended as a comprehensive treatment of all aspects of planning, or to displace the many good volumes on planning by friends and colleagues.

I see this book as a useful treatment of what strategy is, how this interrelates with planning, and how a planning staff can help to make the planning process of its management efficient and effective. These elements are the core. If this core is supplemented (1) by building a familiarity with the leading planning journals (in alphabetical order, **LONG RANGE PLANNING, MANAGERIAL PLANNING,** and **PLANNING REVIEW**), (2) by following the journal footnotes to specialized areas of interest, and (3) by professional interchange with the practitioners in the field, a well-rounded picture will develop rapidly. As a supplement for more rapid learning, or for classroom use, several case books present planning episodes and problems from other companies, and most planning directors can be induced to talk about their own work and experiences, to a group or to a class.

For myself, I want to recognize the degree to which I have learned from all of those who have introduced me to the many facets of planning, strategy and management; in particular from Peter Drucker, who caused me to start on the road of defining my own understanding of the management I was practicing, and from Herb

Grossman, the most stimulating and demanding boss I have ever had, who first exposed me to the multiple aspects of formal and informal planning systems. And then as this book has taken shape, my wife, Margo, has supported the project, accepting it as necessary and important, for all of the hours and days it has taken away from other tasks and from family affairs.

Finally and not least, my thanks to PEI and to Len Parent in particular for his interest in the project, and to the Schwager Fund of the Economics Department of City College for its support.

George Sawyer
Garrison, New York 10524

TABLE OF CONTENTS

Planning - the plan and the process - the planning context - planning as action laid out in advance - levels of planning as levels of management thinking - the planning function - facing problems.

Outline of a strategic plan: summary, background, environment, appraisal, mission, goals, strategy, product programs, forecast, functional plans, resource requirements, financial analysis, realism, alternatives, recommendations - building a simple plan outline - the planning process as a continuous flow - summary.

What is a business? social role, rules → policies - choosing a mission - the mission as a planning tool - the mission of a diverse enterprise - mission statements for conglomerate companies - customer franchises and contractual franchises - keeping the business relevant to its customers.

Two purposes of the goals - goals and goal tradeoffs - unrecognized assumptions: hidden goals, goals with unacceptable consequences, goal conflict - establishing goals - how detailed can goals be? - goal tradeoffs - planning for goals - progress through goals.

vi

PLAN OF THE BOOK

What is planning? Why is it needed? Who does it? What kinds and varieties of planning are there? Among other things this book will discuss the nature and role of planning, of the planning function, and of those who perform it.

Chapter I suggests some of the interrelationships between the levels and varieties of planning. This is as background, so that the necessary planning-for-results orientation can be kept in focus as techniques are considered.

As a step into planning, a plan outline is presented and discussed in Chapter II. The outline is drawn from a strategic plan as the most rounded of the planning processes. It illustrates a useful order in presentation of a plan — but as a general guideline to be varied as appropriate. It presents planning as a process to be captured only in snapshot form at a moment in time and recorded in a document.

The strategic plan outline presented here serves to illustrate a process generic to the various types of planning. And as the various sorts of planning processes have a parallel flow, so do the resulting planning documents have a generic similarity. Discussion of the outline of a strategic plan establishes a general outline of a planning process and of the documents written to record its results.

Two key elements underly a plan and give rise to the strategy. These are the mission, discussed in Chapter III and the goals, discussed in Chapter IV. The mission defines the franchise within which a profitable, socially acceptable business can be built, and the goals define a framework within which the energies of the organization can be mustered and released in the pursuit of the strategy and the execution of the plan. The strategy discussed in Chapter V lays out the elements upon which it depends for any given product or business, and the various sources of profit which effective strategies can tap.

Planning as an effective managerial process depends on many components. One of the most critical is the strategy formulation process. This process is often frustrated by imperfections in the information and perspective of key managers. Chapter VI shows how strategic blindness develops logically from the training of good operating managers, discusses how such problems may be overcome, and defines the elements which should be included in the strategic overview necessary for effective strategy formulation. These elements, which each represent a management task and merit a plan, are discussed individually in Chapters VII to XII. They include plans for the management of social impact, opportunity, course correction, operations, self-renewal, and the information gathering and analysis required to assist the effective functioning of the other elements.

Another major element in business strategy and business management is the proper choice and use of technology. Chapter XIII deals with technology and technical planning and their relationship to the other elements in the planning process. Chapter XIV then extends this to product and market planning, presenting the stages of product differentiation and the levels of focus, the way in which they interact, and how an analysis of competitive action potential can aid in designing a strategy.

Even as a strategy is defined within the strategic overview framework outlined earlier and based on a careful choice of mission and goals, many alternatives remain. Chapter XV discusses the evaluation of strategic alternatives and describes how conceptual strategic models can be used to examine these alternatives, develop their consequences, and refine the process of selection. Another evaluation procedure based on the strategy comparison checklist is also presented. Only after a satisfactory strategy is evaluated and selected can it be concluded that the original choice of mission and goals was realistic, at least in having given rise to a well-defined action plan.

Planning is usually carried out in a major organization through a formal planning system of one or another sort. Chapter XVI discusses some of the elements which determine the appropriate approach to planning and relate it to the other components of the management system.

Line managers must carry out the planning, but in any organization a key staff role makes the system work. Chapter XVII discusses the many ways in which the planning staff can facilitate and, to a degree, oversee the line planning process.

The planning effort has meaning only as it aids in the more active components of the managerial process. This effort is effective only to the degree that it fits the needs of the specific organization and of the managers who are responsible for its operation. Thus the scale and nature of the planning system must be closely keyed to the nature and management style of that specific organization, and Chapter XVIII deals with the parameters of this process.

Just as the strategic overview concept calls for planning for the management of corporate opportunity, these plans must be put into action, through specific decisions, or by delegation to research or other operating units. These actions are elements in an innovation process which must be guided and managed if it is to yield the desired results. While the decisive actions are those of line management, effective staff support is often critical to success. This support can come from specific innovation departments, and from corporate staff. Because of its other central roles and its necessarily broad perspective, the planning function is ideally positioned either to assist R&D in this role, or directly to carry it out, as discussed in Chapter XIX.

Planning is a central, essential process, innately creative in its nature. Chapter XX summarizes the planning role and contribution, and its value-added contribution to the effective management of the business.

CHAPTER I

PLANNING — A MANAGEMENT COMPONENT, AND AN ORGANIZATIONAL ROLE

Planning is a simple, basic process. It involves a cycle of events, as goals are set, means proposed to reach these goals, alternatives evaluated, a route chosen, and a pattern of actions laid out and set into motion. Then as these actions have their effects, other organizations react, facts change, and the course of action must be restated or reaffirmed. This calls for fresh definition of alternatives for reaching these goals from the present position, a fresh choice of route, and a new action program. Thus the cycle repeats, ever varied by new facts and ever similar in its intrinsic nature.

Simple in its essence, planning can have many developments and embodiments. It has given rise to specialized sub-disciplines, such as the Program Evaluation and Review Technique (PERT). Similarly market planning integrates into itself a variety of market research techniques, and production planning can involve sophisticated scheduling algorithms, such as linear programming optimization of oil refinery schedules.

Central to the diversity of planning practice is a universal core tying back to the process of laying out means to achieve the desired ends, and to the basic nature and purpose of the organization. The focus in this book is on that central area.

The practical world is one in which the linkages between the routine operations of the organization and its intended strategic directions are often imperfect. It is a world in which a succession of managers win their positions by achievements in the day-to-day operating world, and then must be caused to learn the need, the value, and the techniques effective planning requires — to increase their managerial effectiveness and to increase their contribution to the management structure.

Planning [1]

Planning is action laid out in advance. It is a central, essential function of management because a manager needs to lay out some pattern of action in order to manage. While managers plan, by habit and by instinct, the functioning of most organizations requires that plans be shared, so that groups of managers actively coordinate their actions toward accomplishment of agreed objec-

1

tives. Thus, planning has become an organizational process, in addition to the individual process of each manager.

For planning to be action laid out in advance, as it is, the plans must have the authority and support of those who will direct the action. These must be the plans of the line managers, the only true planners in any organization. While an important staff role exists in aiding line managers to organize, assemble and coordinate these plans, and in providing the necessary supporting information to these line managers, the staff cannot, by itself, lay out a pattern of action which will be executed. For action to result, the line managers must take personal responsibility for the strategy defined and the issues resolved, and employ their authority to drive the action.

While plans are action laid out in advance, and while the time horizon of plans often extends far into the future, decisions are always made in the present. Line managers live in the present, struggling with the decisions of the day and refusing to be distracted by future decisions which do not yet have to be made. When a decision is needed, managers welcome or even demand information on its future consequences, and normally attempt to take account of a time horizon as long as the futurity of that decision may require, but otherwise their concentration on the present largely keeps them from looking ahead.

The planning and decision process tends to function always in the present, with the relevant future related only to the extent that readily available time and tools permit. If the organization is not to be caught unawares by tomorrow's needs for decisions, those responsible for the planning function must anticipate impending issues needing decision, and gather the information which will be required for intelligent action when these decisions come to term.

The Plan And The Process

One of the important differences between the plan and the process which produces it is that the process flows on from day-to-day as a part of the management operating system (*), while the plan is frozen at a point in time and written. A good plan should be a useful guide to future action, but cannot remain totally valid except briefly because of the rapid rate at which actual events diverge from the norms on which the plan was based. Actual sales may be less or

*MANAGEMENT OPERATING SYSTEM: the system of linkages between different components of the operation by which the different departments and operating units communicate with each other, and by which management directs the operation and receives information on its performance.

greater than forecast, competitive efforts more or less effective than expected, the economy stronger or weaker — each such shift changes the starting point upon which future actions should be based.

Most organizations revise their plans once or more each year, but the plans which result are best considered as normative towards a particular decision, rather than as mandating its blind execution. And while the series of plans generated for a specific business over a period of years often have strong similarities and a consistency in strategy, the details will often be quite different as the needs of different moments in time are reflected by each.

In doing its planning, a management should deal strategically with the longest time horizon it attempts, and should consider planning for a time span long enough to encompass the full futurity of today's decisions. A decision to build a new electric power generating plant may require fifteen years to implement, with payout over the next twenty-five years, thus apparently requiring a forty-year plan. Yet the intense uncertainty of the increasingly future years and the limitations of available planning tools may lead the management to plan for ten years, or even for five, with general projections of trends beyond, and to use this plan as the basis for defining corporate strategy. This strategy may be within the framework of the expected events, or may be made proactive, if it seeks to influence those events.

The purpose is to lay actions out in advance. These actions should be the wisest and best considered that available information will permit. The formulation of a plan requires diversion of valuable managerial time and resources. This diversion of resources should be kept at the minimum effective level.

Procedures and paperwork tend always to grow increasing elaborate if not under careful control. In a well-managed company the pressure is towards careful use of planning time, allowing only that minimum amount of formality necessary to make planning an effective part of the management operating system.

The Planning Context

Planning is an analytical process which encompasses assessment of the future, determination of desired objectives in the context of that future, the development of alternative courses of action to achieve such objectives, and selection of a course (or courses) of action from among such objectives.[2]   --Scott

Planning is action laid out in advance.   --Sawyer

3

Planning is one of the most misunderstood of the corporate staff activities. Even its name contains contradictions, in that planning can only be productive when carried out by line executives. Thus the role of a planning department is not planning, but that of guiding and catalyzing the planning activities of individual line managers and of the total organization through an imaginative combination of staff and consulting (*) activities. Planning staffs do not always clearly define these roles, and often compound the general misunderstanding of their function by their own behavior.

The role of the planning function is difficult and often unpopular because Planning is forever trying to cause the line managers to face awkward problems and uncertainties directly. Planning often questions trusted and timeworn formulas for problem-solving, and frequently precipitates managers into a level of conceptual and strategic (*) thinking a pragmatic day-by-day operative may find thoroughly uncomfortable. These difficulties can be offset eventually when the results of an effective planning effort begin to show. But such efforts have not always been effective, and planning staffs have too often mired down in numerical analysis, formal procedures, and document-writing, and have lost sight of their own purpose.

Planning is an expensive activity, primarily because of the large blocks of managerial and organizational time diverted from other problems and focused on the planning tasks. This is an overhead cost, because it is a prelude to productive managerial activity rather than a part of it. As with any overhead cost, planning effort should be managed so as to get maximum return from the smallest investment effective for the task.

Planning can be a creative, rewarding activity, both to those who help to generate the plans and to the managers who plan, implement, and achieve the results. Planning needs strong, careful management to achieve a larger fraction of its creative potential and to make its maximum contribution to the organization.

Planning As Action Laid Out In Advance

Planning is an essential and integral function of management. It is the primary among the five functions of planning, organizing,

*CONSULTING is a private advisory role in which the first allegiance, within reasonable boundaries of discretion, is to the client, where normal staff activities have primary allegiance to their organizational superior.

*STRATEGIC THINKING, and STRATEGIC PLANNING, deal with the basic definition of an overall approach to a market, a business, an opportunity, or a problem.

4

directing, staffing and controlling.[3] Planning is a necessary step preceding any management action. But like any other management activity, planning should be based on need and justified by results. Otherwise key resources are misdirected or wasted. The need for planning and the results that it can generate are core elements in determining what planning should be done.

The need for planning grows out of the management process, as the need to lay action out in advance, so that decisions, their implementation, and their consequences can more often be visualized together beforehand. The results of planning are in the ability to act with more certainty, that the impacts of that action will include the desired results and consequences. Thus planning is needed for the management action which is its result.

All individuals plan to some degree as a necessary part of their day-to-day activity. The average family dinner is only possible because a family member has planned a menu from available ingredients. In speaking of planning in an organization the tendency is to disregard this elemental planning, which is carried out by all of the individuals in the organization, and by each of the managers for the day-to-day functioning of their units. The tendency is to introduce planning as a new thing and somewhat mysterious, when in fact it is quite familiar but at a less formal level.

The need for planning usually addressed in organizations is a need for organizing, defining, and making explicit this familiar or even instinctive process. This need grows out of the need to bring the management process of the organization out of the individual minds of one or a few leaders and into a forum amongst a management group. If such a need does not exist, planning can be left at the spontaneous and instinctive level.

The reason that the management process in an organization may need to become a matter of discussion amongst a group lies with the growth of organizations and shift of managerial roles. The genius-entrepreneur is a prototype of a manager who needed no formalized planning process.[4] So long as this manager had complete understanding of all issues affecting the business, effective and unquestioned control of its resources, and genius enough to maintain current integration of all of these factors and apply it in moment-to-moment decisions, there was no need for formal planning, and little or no delegation of responsibility to subordinate managers.

The limits on the effectiveness of this type of manager are reached (I) when subordinates must share in defining their own roles, (II) when the collective intelligence of a group is needed to assimilate necessary information and to hammer out an effective strategy, or (III) when a course of action must be reviewed and approved by superiors, directors or financiers. With the increase in the size of organizations, the increase in size of the resource pool required for their operation, increasing demands on management, and the increasing separation between the managerial role and the ownership of the capital, the genius-entrepreneur has largely been displaced by management heirarchies and teams. Management has increasingly become a team activity which requires a shared planning process in order to be effective.

A sharing of information and of objective becomes necessary, among the members of a group of managers and subordinates who are jointly planning. These interpersonal communication processes become the principal vehicle for the collective planning process that governs the direction of the organization.

The requirement for better management is based on the gap between the need and the current performance. The potential for better management is based on a different gap, between the use that is being made of the available resources, and the best use that could be made. In a very profitable organization additional potential may go long untapped. But when an organization is under pressure, even delivery of the full potential may not be sufficient to keep the enterprise afloat. Planning can aid in determining both need and potential, so that programs have some realism, and so that some effort is made to tap the full potential of the resources.

There are many ways that a planning effort can act as an aid and a catalyst to better management. This is its sole justification, and the achievement of better management leading to better organizational performance is the desired outcome. Results-oriented planning can mean only planning geared to achieving the best possible management of the unit or the enterprise. Other than in its translation into effective action the planning process has no meaning. Management needs action laid out in advance in order that it choose its actions wisely. Planning is justified to the extent that it contributes on a cost/benefit basis to creation of an improved pattern of actions.

Levels Of Planning As Levels Of Management Thinking

Many kinds of planning are needed by different kinds and levels of organizational units. Operating plans, marketing plans, financial plans, development plans, diversification plans, strategic plans, and many other types have been defined. They interrelate in a simple way, each adding a facet to a total plan for the enterprise.

Planning as a part of the management process must be appropriate to that process. Operating management needs operating plans, financial management needs financial plans, and each plan has its set of goals. Goal management in any plan at any level has a component that continually verifies the relationship of that effort to the corporate whole, as a part of keeping its effective organizational role. Thus production management not only plans to operate the production centers efficiently, but also to relate their output to the needs of the other parts of the enterprise. It continually verifies the strategic direction of its efforts, if it is being managed effectively.

At the highest level of the business unit or of the total enterprise and oriented toward a global view of the internal and external environment is the strategic planning. This is a top management function which gives direction to the total organization and to its components, and provides the basis for derivative plans at the lower levels.

The Planning Function

The operation of the planning function should be appropriate to the specific management process, at the operating levels and at the strategic level. It contributes best by facilitating their integration into a total framework as an effective component in managerial action. The emphasis is on gearing the planning process to the level at which management is prepared to make effective use of the insights the process can generate.

Where there is a tendency among purists to emphasize strategic planning as a separate form, a more realistic approach is to emphasize at all times and at all planning levels the need to render effective aid to the actual management process. This is also a means to the eventual evolution of that process to the highest level of strategic thinking appropriate to the specific business circumstances. Line managers tend to learn first to live in the day-to-day world, and the step up to a strategic level of thinking may sometimes be difficult in the absence of an organized planning process.

Any step helping the individual manager to develop a better personal planning process to deal with his or her operating problems is also a step towards that manager's education and training. The logical consequences of such education is an evolution towards strategic planning at a level which fully integrates the different elements of the enterprise. But logical as that evolution may be, the human learning process is such that often the individual managers must rediscover this evolution in an operating environment.

This sounds a lot like reinventing the wheel, and it is. It differs in that the performance pressures and practical training of operating management often bars application of theoretical concepts based on experience elsewhere until these concepts have been freshly proven on home ground. Those in the planning function may experience massive frustration with this individualized learning process, but the role either of staff or of consultant is one of working to make the line effective, and the energy must go to new and better techniques to make this learning process swifter and more efficient.

Thus the different levels of planning in an organization often are also different levels of thinking and of education in planning techniques for the line managers. The role of the planning function is to aid the line in getting its planning done, starting at the level of greatest perceived planning needs and building up to a more comprehensive and strategic level as the self-teaching of the line managers and the successes of the planning efforts justify that extension.

Facing Problems

It may seem that such an approach allows the neglect of urgent problems of the enterprise, as seen by the staff, and to some extent this criticism is justified. However, nothing prevents moving directly by convincing management of the urgency of such problems, except that this may not be easy.

Sometimes without a coordinated and effective operating structure and the discipline of good operating plans managers are reluctant to acknowledge and to grapple with problems at the strategic level at all. After all, a good strategy requires ability to implement the action selected. If a good strategic plan is not already supported by strong management capabilities able to integrate their efforts in accomplishment of the task, these capabilities must quickly be constructed or else the plan will fail.

To put this more succinctly, it profits the planning function little to have insights that line management does not both share and carry into action. The line managers who make the decisions and spend the money must achieve or accept the strategic insights, or else they are wasted. To be effective planning must cause its insights to be accepted and shared, or else to be discovered independently by the key line managers.

FOOTNOTES

¹This section is derived from "Planning Viewpoint: Top Management," **Planning**

Review, pp. 37-38, and the executive commentary written for the planning chapter in *Management: Making Organizations Perform,* by Archie B. Carroll, et al, Mac-Millan, New York, 1981.

[2]Brian W. Scott, *Long Range Planning In American Industry,* American Management Association, New York, 1965, p. 21.

[3]Harold Koontz & Cyril O'Donnell, *Principles of Management,* Fifth Edition, McGraw-Hill, New York, 1972, p. 46ff.

[4]Robert F. Stewart, et al, *The Strategic Plan,* Long Range Planning Service Report No. 168, Stanford Research Institute, Menlo Park, California, 1963.

CHAPTER II

PROFILE OF A PLAN

One of the characteristics of the planning process is its pervasiveness. Every place that major operations are being carried out under the direction of a management, planning is occurring and this planning is following the same general framework. While in individual cases this planning may be disorganized or uncoordinated, the underlying management process has this common trend.

Outline Of A Strategic Plan

To aid in recognizing the general characteristics of this underlying process and applying them to a particular planning problem a useful outline is shown in Figure II-1 and discussed below. While there is no requirement that any specific outline be used, these elements will be found in some form in any good strategic plan.

Figure II-1

OUTLINE OF A STRATEGIC PLAN

1. Executive Summary
2. Background
3. Environment
4. Business Appraisal
5. Mission
6. Goals
7. Strategy
8. Product or Service Programs
9. Forecast
10. Functional Plans
11. Resource Requirements
12. Financial Analysis
13. Realism
14. Alternatives
15. Recommendations

EXECUTIVE SUMMARY. Each plan should start with a brief section designed to give the essence of the plan and its recommendations in a quick capsule for the busy reader. At first the concept of a Summary section is a disturbing one to some managers, who would prefer that the reader be led through a logical sequence as the plan is constructed. Good literary and dramatic form would call for careful articulation of the argument, a good logic flow, and even an element of suspense before the final capsule of the plan is unfolded.

Unfortunately, real world executives often lose patience with good literary presentation form. To save time for accomplishment managers must curtail time spent on reading. Some follow the practice advocated by the late President Kennedy, of skimming the contents briefly to decide whether a document is worth reading. Others simply try a page or two, and then reconsider. If the subject is not of personal importance or if the first pages have not justified interest, the executive goes on to other issues and the plan is shelved or discarded.

It is strongly recommended that a strategic plan or any other plan start with a good, brief summary. Since the larger part of the readership will never go beyond the summary, it should contain the substance of what they need to know.

Given a good summary, those few who have great interest or something at stake will read the plan carefully. They may read it for information, as the basis for their approval, as a means to prepare a brief in its support, or as critical opponents searching for flaws. The body of a good plan will receive serious and critical readership, but only from a relatively small group of friends and enemies. This body should be substantial if it is to withstand analysis, and honestly supportive of the statements that the summary contains.

BACKGROUND. This is an important section, too often omitted. A plan starts from a context growing out of the history of the enterprise. The firm is controlled by managers with individual personalities, some have taken positions on issues, and in any ongoing management process a history of successes and failures is already established. The purpose of a Background section in the plan is briefly to state the context in which the plan is being constructed and presented. This is a point of departure, with a set of assumptions about where the business has been and the kinds of stresses and strains which must be considered in planning the next steps forward.

One of the important things about a Background section is that not all of the readers will agree with it. If a manager feels that his planning is heavily constrained by the need to make use of available plant capacity, it is important to say so. If a shortage of cash requires delay in previously established plans for increasing inventories, this should be stated. If these assumptions are not stated, then the chance to reinforce or to change them may be missed. If members of the management group which is reviewing the plan disagree with these assumptions, they can say so, and perhaps new programs will become possible as a result.

In any case it is important to state this context, to refresh the memories of those who may not have thought about this business as an entity since the previous plan was presented and to provide background for new managers. Thus, each reader will start the plan with an awareness of the boundaries and limitations used by the planning group and built into the structure.

ENVIRONMENT. Each plan has a surrounding context. Businesses are affected by recessions, earthquakes, wars, disasters, social stress, market conditions, competitive actions, inflation, taxes, and a host of other external factors. Obvious though many of these factors may be, they are often missed by managers so involved in the day-to-day routine that they cannot find the time to stop and think about the world in which their business functions. A brief Environment section provides the discipline of an organized statement in a context appropriate to the plan.

In a strategic plan the Environment section should survey the environment briefly and comprehensively, but should only devote time to careful development where a particular factor is likely to affect corporate decisions now or in the near future. A survey of environmental factors often starts with the likely impacts on the business of (I) developments in the political and regulatory environment, (II) social forces and economic trends, (III) changing technology, and (IV) developments in the competitive environment. Also it often includes (V) a profile of the actual markets in which the business operates. In some cases the ecological factors influencing the business are of such importance as also to be discussed separately. As its contribution to the plan, the Environment section highlights the most critical sensitivities and vulnerabilities of this business to the world around it.

BUSINESS APPRAISAL. This is a short section encapsulating a summary of the business situation. Given the background as stated and the present and projected environment as the planning group sees it, what is a realistic assessment of the business outlook? The purpose of the Appraisal section is to sharpen and converge the analysis drawn out of the Background and Environment, and to underscore those key questions which provide a backdrop for the plan which will follow.

MISSION. The Mission is a statement of the role in which a business hopes and plans to serve society. As a profit-seeking entity, a business unit can survive only by providing goods or services to some segment of society at a price greater than the cost. In order for the necessary price to be paid, the purchasers must see value in the purchases greater than the purchasing power which must be surrendered to obtain them. The business must perform some valuable role, through offering goods or services in which buyers see value greater than the cost, or it cannot survive. This role, in which it can find the basis for its pursuit of profit, is its mission. Thus the mission is also that franchise in the market place on which a continuing business is based.

While the mission of a business may derive more or less spontaneously during its early struggles, that mission or franchise needs to be thoroughly understood, and to be changed only intentionally and with care, lest the commercial basis of success be undermined in the course of some expansion. The nature and definition of the mission can become complex, particularly in a diverse enterprise, as discussed in more detail in Chapter III.

GOALS. Goals — or objectives — are a necessary precursor to any serious plan for accomplishments. These goals may be informal or formal. When the management of an enterprise has been informal in the past, the planning group will often find that goals have never been made explicit. Frequently a major benefit of a more organized planning process is that members of the organization are led to recognize and share a statement of their goals for the first time.

To reemphasize: A plan is action laid out in advance. The action is aimed at accomplishment. A statement of what the business is trying to accomplish is a statement of its goals. If goals cannot be found and stated, then there is hardly any point in trying to plan actions.

Where the mission is a statement of the service to society for which the business is designed, the goals are specific ends to be achieved by business action. Here and in any plan, goals occur in heirarchy, where the highest level is the statement of overall accomplishment which is being attempted. Where one business may strive to increase market share, another may set its goals in terms of sales and profits. The Avis "we try harder" campaign carried with it a clearcut goal of challenging Hertz and becoming number one instead of number two in the car rental business.

As discussed further in Chapter IV, the purpose of a Goals section in a plan is to draw out a concise statement of what the following programs of action are designed to accomplish. This makes the logic much clearer to the executives who must approve the plan, as well as aiding the planning group itself in developing and communicating that logic.

STRATEGY. From a set of goals which are often somewhat abstract, the next step is to their means of achievement. Given that market share is to be increased, how should this be done? Of the several alternatives, is the best option a major promotion campaign? A different method of distribution? A radical price cut? From these and yet other alternatives a basic approach to goal achievement must be selected in order for the planning to proceed. This major approach is the strategy which this business will follow in striving to achieve its goals.

Strategy as a term comes from the military. And the analogy between a business plan and a battle plan has often been elaborated. Just as in planning the conquest of France the German general staff defined a series of alternative strategies and prepared a complete battle plan for each strategy before making its choice, it is often necessary to consider the results various business alternatives might yield, before a specific strategy can be chosen and put in motion. Chapter V discusses strategy in more detail, and Chapter XIV develops the concept of a strategic model as a means of contrasting the likely results from different strategies before choosing one and committing resources to its execution.

PRODUCT OR SERVICE PROGRAMS. When a strategy has been selected, the next step is to block out the major action areas around which the implementation plans should be organized. These often represent groups of products or services — hence the term Product or Service Programs. It is common to find that products in a product line occur in families which should be logically related in their planning and marketing, more than other products in the line.

For example, when Miles Laboratories added Alka Seltzer Plus and Alka II to its product offerings, this joint use of the Alka Seltzer franchise, trade name and product image brought the need for an interrelationship of the marketing efforts of these three products. Similarly, in a mail order catalog from Sears or Wards the products are grouped together. The buying staff can plan for appliances, televisions, power tools, or women's shoes as groups of products in such a product line.

In moving from strategy to forecasted accomplishments the

14

forecasting can best be organized in a logical framework built on natural relationships. Definition of these natural relationships as the basis for product programs is a useful prelude to forecasting, and aids in developing a consistent set of actions to implement the chosen strategy.

FORECAST. From the Product or Service Programs as developed from the strategy, what will the output be? In the case of a strategic plan for a business selling products or services, the forecast is for sales or other revenues. This is based on the number of units which will be sold and the price which will be charged. Where products are leased or installed on a shared-revenue basis, the terms of the forecast may be somewhat different. In any case the Forecast section is intended as a simple statement of the revenue the business can be expected to generate as a result of the plan presented here for approval.

FUNCTIONAL PLANS. The strategy, as broken into Product Programs and developed into a forecast, is a projection of results which can only be achieved if the necessary components of the organization function together in a coordinated way. This means that each of the functional areas which has a role in implementing the strategy must itself develop a plan for this role, with its own set of goals and strategy. This section of the strategic plan is intended to present these functional plans in their relationship to the strategy and forecast.

Detailed functional planning is often necessary. However, the corresponding component of the strategic plan, whether it be for marketing, manufacturing, distribution, research, engineering or another function, is usually limited to a brief summary supported elsewhere by a separate plan elaborated to any required amount of detail. Production plans often are carried out in great detail, where the strategic plan need only contain a brief summary integrated with the related functional efforts.

RESOURCE REQUIREMENTS. The functional plans become real and meaningful to management only when they also are related to a statement of what the effort will cost. If an expanded program requires more people, or new capital commitments, or some other change in resource needs, the Resource Requirements section is designed to show this as well as the planned use of existing resources. The resource requirements of all of the functional plans should add together to a statement of total resources required to accomplish the strategic plan which is being presented.

15

The Resource Requirements section will largely be cast in financial terms, but it is useful also to include other statements of the demands on scarce resources. For instance, many managements find it useful to have a tabulation of the numbers and levels of people required to staff each function, or the loading on a key item of equipment.

FINANCIAL ANALYSIS. From the Resource Requirements, which show a full statement of the costs of the business and from the forecast, which projects its revenues, an income statement and balance sheet can be constructed and examined. The Financial Analysis section is intended to present and analyze this income statement and balance sheet, in terms of rates of return, resource demands, and general soundness of the approach. Often the first analysis of a new plan shows that it is less than satisfactory, and requires a reappraisal of forecasts and use of resources before the plan can be completed and submitted.

REALISM. A plan is of necessity built on assumptions. These assumptions should be chosen with care and presented as made. At the end of the planning process, however, it is useful both to the group doing the planning and to those who must approve the results if the composite of those assumptions is reviewed for realism.

The planning group should not be allowed to make assumptions and then disclaim them. However, given that the best assumptions have been made at every stage, there still is room for a composite judgment as to whether the probabilities of a plan working out well are good or bad, due to the risk of events from outside of the plan interfering with its progress. The purpose of this Realism section is to give the next levels of management an appraisal from the planning group, particularly since others will raise these same uncertainties as issues. For control of the discussion process it is best to identify and address known uncertainties openly, both to show that they have been considered, and to present these uncertainties from the perspective that the planning group prefers to use.

ALTERNATIVES. Almost every strategy and almost every plan is based on the choice amongst alternatives. The normal human process is to seize immediately on the alternative which seems best, but in establishing the credibility of a plan it is important to establish that other alternatives are know to exist and were, in fact, considered. The purpose of an Alternatives section is to catalog some of these briefly and to mention the reasons for their discard.

16

Often a proposed course of action is strengthened by such a review, because the only alternatives are so unpalatable.

Another part of the value of an Alternatives section is to reduce the psychological pressure on top management which a good, well-presented plan may tend to create. The thrust of a strong plan toward the chosen alternative may be so powerful as to create sales resistance, as the management begins to feel as if its approval were being demanded. It is useful to remind top management that there are alternatives, that they are not "forced" to approve the plan, although all of the other courses of action may be less attractive. This review of alternatives aids top management in becoming more comfortable with the strategy and recommendations of a good plan, and moves these managers towards its approval.

RECOMMENDATIONS. The energy and exposure required in laying out a plan and circulating it to top management is a part of a program for accomplishment. The plan should be a means to obtaining top management endorsement of the action program. The Recommendations section summarizes briefly the specific actions which should be taken and requests approval. If the plan has been well-constructed, these recommendations, which were presented briefly in the Executive Summary, will have developed from the logic of the flow of the plan, and will stand out as good candidates for executive approval when the plan is reviewed.

Building A Simple Plan Outline

The preceding section has presented fifteen elements that a strategic plan should include. Most other plans should include them also. These elements were presented in a natural order, and could become fifteen chapters in a plan. But often such a direct application would be too formal or stereotyped.

While major planning documents are produced in many corporations, and while these fifteen elements form a logical, well-balanced and effective structure for a substantive literary effort, the theme in this book is to minimize formality, and to give extra emphasis to those elements most useful to a specific management at a specific time. In many cases a short, well-conceived plan will fit the need better than a massive work, and the savings are very great. A good, short plan is more likely to be read and used, and as such is better able to return the value on which the value-added planning process must be justified.

The point is that the fifteen elements recited here can easily be combined in a number of ways, and should be combined where this aids in achieving a more brief and more effective presentation. Thus, functional plans and resource requirements can often be discussed together, or mission and goals. But the discipline of carrying out planning effectively requires that the concept of each element be adequately included, even though no formal chapter heading may be necessary.

The Planning Process As A Continuous Flow

After all, the planning process is a continuum. Even a segmentation into fifteen elements is somewhat artificial. And, the nature of planning is such that often the analysis of the issues and synthesis of possible solutions must cycle through these elements again and again before the projected profits and returns have the best possible relationship with inputs and investments.

The planning process is a flow process which cycles through its various articulations as decisions occur, sales are made, and as new facts are gathered. As such the planning process is an essential component of the management operating system, and should be made to flow as simply and naturally as possible.

The planning process also produces plans. A plan can be visualized as a snapshot of this process, based on the relationship between the elements of the business at one moment in time and projecting the evolution of this relationship into the future. Just as different snapshots of two friends having a conversation may differ substantially in details as the conversation evolves, so may two plans developed from the same process for the same business at different times.

Figure II-2
Two Friends in Conversation

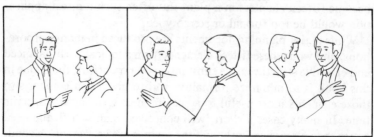

A well-conceived plan defines directions and general relationships, and under all but the most turbulent conditions these relationships should change only slowly. But, the details of a specific plan are usually misleading to some degree, because these details were determined by special conditions in that moment when the

18

snapshot was taken. Thus plans tend to be most effective in defining strategies and general principles of action, and least effective in predicting or controlling the details of actions to be taken at a specific moment in the future.

Summary

In the general case, all plans are to a certain extent analogs, in that there is a context, goals are necessary, a strategy, and a set of actions, all with forecasted results and projected costs. As these are balanced, they lead to outcomes analysis and recommendations for action. The outline developed in this chapter is that of a strategic plan, but as suggested initially the outline has a general applicability, even though in some planning problems different sections will need more or less development and must fit the process of the business — for example, in some activities where the output is not quantitative the forecast must be in qualitative terms also.

The summary thought here is that planning is a process with a logical sequence of elements which should be reflected in any good plan. The outline above represents one way in which these elements can be put together in a useful and constructive way.

CHAPTER III

THE MISSION, AS A CLAIM ON A FRANCHISE

What Is A Business?

Two important characteristics of a business often are unrecognized.First, its economic existence can only be sustained by social accomplishments. Second, it has almost no pre-existing pattern for its conduct. Management must create rules or policies to govern this conduct, and the chance of success for the business is determined by how well this definition of policies is performed.

SOCIAL ROLE. A business — or any other organization — exists for some purpose. And the purpose is not merely "to make money" — that comes later and easily, if the real business purpose is satisfactorily fulfilled. Henry Ford started out to build and sell cars. He learned how to do it very well, and became rich and powerful — but that was not the purpose of the Ford Motor Company, even if Ford had desired wealth and power from the beginning.

A business — or any other organization — is created for a social role, and in this role the Ford Motor Company was attempting to supply as large a share as possible of the nation's need for personal transportation. Only by definition and fulfillment of this social role did it create the potential for making profits. Ford's success illustrates the relationship between economic gain and social fulfillment on which our industrial society is built.

A business is an economic entity. A corporation, as the most common embodiment through which major business is conducted, is "an artificial being created by law," in the words of John Marshall's famous Supreme Court decision. It has no substance, but the law gives it life as if it were an individual. Its essence is defined by its income statement, balance sheet, and other measures of its economic value and performance. Money is the language of the firm.

Because a corporation or other business is an economic entity, it has difficulties in recognizing values that are other than economic — it lives or dies by its economic performance. But its economic performance depends first on its defining an adequate and worthwhile social role, and then on effective performance of this role. To succeed, it must accomplish social ends — as represented by the role it has chosen — by economic means, even though the social and the economic often fit together only imperfectly.

To a surprisingly large extent other types of organizations — governmental, charitable, not-for-profit — are also constructed with an essentially economic nature. They are similarly described by income statement and balance sheet, and almost always have difficulty in transition from the economic means to the social ends which are their purpose.

RULES►POLICIES. The other related dimension of the nature of a business is that it comes into being with no rules for its conduct. Any other individual is born into a society which prescribes acceptable behavior in detail, and that individual can live out his or her life according to these prescriptions. But the individual business is born without a code describing what it should do.

The business has many rules describing what it should not do. Society in its role as the law-giver and rule-maker creates regulations of the "thou shalt not" variety in large numbers. But the "thou shalt" component is missing almost completely.

A business can attempt to succeed by looking at what other businesses do, and imitating them. Many small businesses operate in this way. But major businesses generally cannot exist by imitation of others — the members of each management must plan out what they feel that they should do and do it, if they hope to endure.

The point of this is to emphasize that management is in the position of making up its own rules as it goes along — after giving heed to society's "thou shalt nots" if it wishes to stay out of legal difficulty. And the premium on successful invention of new rules, of new approaches to a market place or to a customer need, of rules that will give a worthwhile competitive advantage — this premium is very large.

Of course, this successful invention of new rules comes naturally from the planning process through the definition of a mission, of specific goals which represent progress in fulfilling that mission, and a worthwhile strategy for moving toward those goals. As it defines this strategy and commits itself to the pattern in which it wishes to operate, that management makes policy — that is, it sets down some of the rules of conduct specifying how it hopes to operate its business. But first it selects a specific mission, and that is the subject of the balance of this chapter.

Choosing A Mission

The reason that competitive pursuit of profit within socially defined boundaries is healthy is that it builds a competition to serve the needs of society well, and at minimum cost. But the root of success is in the service, and the profit follows only if society finds the service desirable, and as meriting a price greater than the cost.

The basis for success of a business is the franchise it establishes as a servant of society's needs. Within the boundaries of that franchise it seeks to build its sales position and to garner its profits. The mission is the territory a business maps out for itself, where the franchise is established by recognition from others. In many markets the franchise is simply the consumer recognition, loyalty, and purchase pattern built up over time.

In other markets the franchise is also controlled by contract with a purveyor of products or services, such as General Motors, Carvel, or United Business Services, who franchise automobile distributorships, ice cream stores, and business services, respectively. Or, the franchise may be the result of government action, as in the case of the license for a television station or the local monopoly of a regulated utility company. The franchise is a vested position based on past actions or contracts, where the mission is an expression of management intent. This intent will result in the building or maintenance of a franchise if that intent is translated into effective action programs.

Franchises do not endure forever. The market place may or may not respect a vested position. New offerings challenge brand loyalties, business leaks from one franchised distributor to another, and monopolies are invaded, as when the growth of interstate trucking circumvented the regulated freight monopoly of the railroads. The franchise is the starting point based on past actions, and the mission expresses the direction towards which present energies are to be directed. Pursuit of this mission will bring changes, as successful or unsuccessful actions in the present reinforce or attenuate the franchise accumulated from the past.

A business defines its own mission through its actions. The degree of recognition this pattern of actions receives in the marketplace is reflected in the nature and strength of the franchise which results.

The Mission As A Planning Tool

The mission is the defined effort to find a social role — a role in the service of society — which will support a profitable business. If an inventor builds, patents and successfully markets a better mouse trap, the result is a mouse trap business. Underlying this business is

22

a mission of providing householders and others with an improved mouse-control device.

A mouse trap is a product which society finds valuable. A mouse trap which is viewed by potential purchasers as a superior product in relation to its cost is likely to find a ready market. The purchasers will not care whether or not the inventor has defined the mission of the mouse trap business. And most often the new single-product business grows in a largely unplanned and expedient way as it struggles to become established.

But as the now-successful mouse trap business moves into the future, it faces Drucker's "What is my business?" question.[1] That is, what is the effective role in the market place for this business as it grows and diversifies? A mouse trap company could continue in that single business — but if so it will face the inevitable maturation of the market as others find ways to imitate the product, and with possible competitive inroads from newer and better traps.

Most successful businesses seek to add other products or services to broaden the economic base and to add sales and profits. A mouse trap company could develop and sell other types of traps. It might define a mission such as "to provide quality traps for the nation's needs." But, where mouse traps and rat traps are often similar in design, muskrat traps and bear traps would use different materials and require different fabricating techniques. Where mouse traps and rat traps are often retail hardware items, traps for fur-bearing animals move through different distribution channels, and coyote and other traps for pest control may invoke yet other specialized market routes. In addition to animal traps there are bird traps, and fish traps, each distributed in its own way.

The steps a business takes as it moves into new areas bring problems and challenges, and these should be evaluated in advance. While no business needs to enter all areas or face all challenges, it must choose some of them in order to grow, or to escape the limits of the life cycle of its first successful product.

Most companies have a variety of choices for this growth. The mouse trap company could develop markets beyond the borders of the U.S., in a quest for a major share of the global mouse trap market. Or a mouse trap company could look at pest control and enter that business. This would mean mastering the use of various poisons and chemical agents in addition to traps, and training a field force of agents who could operate independently on the customer's premises, exterminating pests and taking responsibility for the effectiveness of the job and for any related consequences. This business could be limited to mouse control, or extended to rat control, cockroach control, and termite control — each invoking a new series of techniques, actions, and consequences.

The initial choice suggested here is between a mission of providing products for catching animals and pests, starting with the mouse trap and broadening in some appropriate pattern, or a mission of providing the service of pest removal, starting with mice — or of embracing both missions. A secondary choice is how far to extend the business geographically — locally, regionally, nationally or internationally. There is no specific right or wrong set of decisions, but the skills requirements and exposures of product and service businesses are quite different, and extending marketing into new areas and distribution channels makes new demands.

What the statement of mission is, is a statement of what management is really trying to accomplish, in terms of service to a particular segment of society, as its basis for a profitable business. It is an important planning tool because, correctly stated, it defines key and crucial boundaries. Otherwise these boundaries may be transgressed and the basic franchise seriously eroded before management is aware of the problem.

For example, a number of successful retail operations have had the experience of adding individually profitable new lines one after another but with disastrous impact on total sales — because the added products changed the total retail image until the store lost the core customer group whose loyalty represented the basic franchise of the business. Sears managers have given parallel reasons for shifts back to earlier marketing strategies, and some analysts have found indications that problems of this type contributed to the past losses at A&P.

A going business exists because it has established a franchise in the marketplace. Management needs an understanding of the nature, boundaries, and probable durability of that franchise. The mission statement represents a distillation of that understanding. This statement can either be congruent with the existing franchise, and based on perpetuating it, or somewhat different from the present franchise and likely to bring franchise extensions or shifts as it is implemented.

The Mission Of A Diverse Enterprise

The most straightforward mission concepts are those tying the mission of a specific business unit to market needs and to its potential franchise. This leaves open the question of the manner in which a mission can be stated and made effective for a more diverse enterprise. The answer is direct: the mission is a statement of service to society which, if performed effectively, will lead to the development of a franchise. Therefore, a diverse enterprise can deal with its mission only by building upon business elements which have the potential for market recognition and franchise development.

The simplest level of diversity is of a national business which must develop its franchise in each local area. Thus ARA Services, as a major operator of institutional restaurants and cafeterias, gains little recognition from those who purchase its meals in a college cafeteria from the fact that it also feeds the Pentagon in Washington, D.C. At the local level its mission must be performed and its franchise built by each restaurant or cafeteria separately. However, during negotiations for the all-important contract to operate the college cafeteria, ARA can derive great credibility as a bidder from its national stature. The point is that the common ties amongst the elements of a diverse enterprise, while important to the strength and success of the enterprise, may or may not be relevant to the building of a franchise in the local marketplace.

The students in one college cafeteria are likely neither to know nor to care that ARA operates cafeterias in other colleges. In the case of a service business such as that of ARA, the underlying business may be homogeneous — in this case, based on providing meals in a certain price range to specific elements of the public on a contract basis — and yet the market franchise must be developed independently in each area based on local performance.

Another increasingly national enterprise is the Herman's sporting goods chain. While it has built its ties with local customers around each store, the population mobility and media patterns for its advertising encourage the development of an entire metropolitan area, with stores located at convenient intervals throughout that region. Between metropolitan areas franchise ties are much weaker. Thus the growth from local to national markets is largely on a region-by-region basis.

The parent of Herman's is W. R. Grace, a major multinational enterprise, and Herman's growth from region to region has been accelerated by the availability of Grace capital and other resources. Yet the identification of Herman's with a larger enterprise does not contribute to its rate of market penetration and franchise development because the W. R. Grace identity is not particularly relevant to Herman's market place.

The definition of mission and franchise by large and diverse enterprises is complex because of the tendency of the identity of the parent organization to be more or less distant from the actual marketplace, as Grace is from Herman's. In defining its mission to include providing a variety of products for the consumer marketplace, as Grace management seems to have done, the corporation has chosen an approach to the marketplace where the franchise development process is individual, for each subsidiary, rather than a collective process for the entire consumer-oriented portion of the Grace organization.

A few years ago Standard Oil of New Jersey, anxious to develop a clearer national identity for its operations, created the Exxon trade name. Then Esso, Humble, and Standard of New Jersey's other marketing companies all shifted to this single national sales identity, which could be supported by both regional and national promotions. The Exxon campaign was focused on unifying national promotion of a single line of products, so that a stronger franchise could be built and maintained.

Other major consumer marketers have also built the corporate identity where possible, but none-the-less the marketing pull of major brand names such as Jello and Maxwell House are often more important as the basis for the market franchise than the identity of General Foods as the parent.

General Electric is an example of a diverse enterprise which has built a strong corporate identity and carried it into the marketplace of each of its products, where ITT had tended to submerge its identity behind that of its subsidiaries until recently. This is not to suggest that either approach is right or wrong, only that widely different sorts of linkages between the corporate mission and the franchise or franchises which develop can be found in successful current corporate practice.

Mission Statements For Conglomerate Companies

If a conglomerate enterprise wishes to operate on the basis that "we will buy and manage any profitable company which can be made to yield an attractive return," this reduces the potential corporate mission to the level of "we will require (among other things) that the enterprises we buy have or establish missions leading to sound and sustaining franchises in their marketplaces." The corporate identity without any specific service focus can have no independent mission — or social justification — but it can find both through the missions of its subsidiaries.

Between the pure conglomerate enterprise and the marketplace is a considerable distance. A more focused corporation such as W. R. Grace may have businesses concentrated in consumer products, chemicals and other areas, in the way that General Foods concentrates on certain types of consumer products; both can define their corporate missions around specified kinds of service to the chosen groups of customers, but are likely to achieve their franchise largely through subsidiary or brand identities.

26

Until recently, Avon had focused its efforts more sharply, in that it had only sold through its own representatives. Thus, in spite of the size of the enterprise and diversity of the product line, the mission had been carefully limited to the service of the customers and customer needs which could be reached through this channel. A strong corporate market franchise has grown up as a result of the success of this product line, and Avon has undertaken a mission and built a franchise into which it can integrate its major stream of new products. Most other enterprises of equal size must achieve their missions less directly, as General Foods and W. R. Grace do, or even entirely by derivative performance, as in the case of a pure conglomerate.

It is also true that the dimensions of the management task undertaken by these different corporations is quite different. Each different sort of franchise has its own management requirements, and the mixed success of its competitors suggests that the Avon franchise based on direct sale to consumers may be a difficult one to manage successfully. However, the management of an assortment of different franchises is also a task with difficulties of its own, and a part of the problems some conglomerates have had may trace to special challenges in managing entirely through derived franchises.

Again, there is no one way that is right, or wrong, except as it matches to the resources, including management capability, of a given corporation. Thus, Avon, which has had outstanding success in one major franchise area, has recently been exploring diversification through other marketing channels. The correctness of this course of action will be determined over time by the results achieved. The only comment possible in advance of these results is that, in taking this direction, Avon chose to add somewhat to the complexity of its management task.

Customer Franchises And Contractual Franchises

Where ARA Services renders food service to a particular population group, it does so under the terms of a contract with the college or other institution which desires these services. This contract is in effect a franchise, entitling and requiring ARA to supply food under specific conditions. Generically, the franchise entitling and requiring Consolidated Edison to supply electricity to the City of New York is very similar, or the agreement between General Motors and a Chevrolet dealer entitling and requiring that dealer to sell automobiles in a specified manner.

These are all very real franchises in the legal sense, but differ to some extent from the franchise a corporation builds in the market place by effective service of customer needs. ARA needs both types of franchise for its success. That is, it needs the feeding contract for the facility, plus at least the passive consent of the public which buys and eats the food. Otherwise, the contract would be terminated and awarded elsewhere.

A Chevrolet dealer must also have an effective franchise with the local public. Otherwise, they will buy another make of car, or else trade with another Chevrolet dealer in some nearby community.

The Consolidated Edison monopoly is stronger, in that it is more difficult for individual members of the affected public to do without electricity or to obtain it elsewhere. But while difficult, this is not always impossible. Several major New York City office buildings have installed their own generating equipment, Con Ed has been required to accommodate its services to provide backup as necessary for smaller buildings with wind-powered and solar generating systems, and several suburban communities have actively considered bypassing Con Ed and buying their power elsewhere.

A contract or other official statement of franchise is parallel to the actual commercial franchise developed in the marketplace, and the interest of the marketer is in making them more or less congruent. That is, the business needs to build ties with customers which support the legal franchise. The relevance to definition of a business or corporate mission is that if the mission is not aimed at developing the underlying franchise, and if effective programs in support of that mission are not designed and implemented, then the franchise represented by the legal contract may be withdrawn, bypassed, or otherwise lose its meaning.

Keeping The Business Relevant To Its Customers

The importance of the mission statement is as a reference point for the orientation of the efforts of the business. Managers will and should become absorbed in the achievement of their goals, many of which will be short-term and materialistic. And the goals will be the focus around which corporate strategy is conceived. But since the success of the business requires a social role with an economic justification, and since management goals usually do not include this social area, the risk is that actions taken in pursuit of the goals inadvertently jeopardize social justification and the franchise of the business.

In addition, a careful mission statement tends to clarify the issues as to where the strengths of the business are or should be, and as to the deeper implications of the various strategic options as product or service or market extensions are proposed for the existing line.

FOOTNOTES
[1]Peter Drucker, THE PRACTICE OF MANAGEMENT, Harper & Row, New York, 1953.

CHAPTER IV

PLANNING FOR GOALS[1]

The goals of an organization are those achievements towards which management wants the organization to strive as it seeks to fulfill its mission. These goals occur in a heirarchy. The major goals form the overall umbrella directing and focusing organizational effort, and the more minor goals the subsidiary targets of the various organizational components.

All organizations have goals. Where an organization operates without stated goals, the pattern of action implies them, even though these goals might not receive full management approval if explicitly stated.

Two Purposes Of The Goals

A primary purpose of an organization's goals is to provide the basis for designing strategy, thus making possible plans and action — the strategy provides a road-map for progress in achieving the goals, and defines directions for action. Goals may be general or detailed, many or few, according to the terms in which management wishes to describe its business. For example, many goal statements include sales, profits and market share.

The second major purpose of a set of goals is to engage the imagination of the organization and to permit the constructive application of their inherent energy and enthusiasm. Most people desire meaningful activity, and try to reinforce the importance of their own individual activities as a member of an organization by identifying with its larger goals. Management aids in this process by defining and sharing its goals for that organization.

If the organization's goals are vague or unknown, the members of the organization will develop their own set of goals — identifying with and devoting their energy to the creation of the best corporate library, research department, or union local — rather than unifying in the pursuit of corporate targets. A clear set of goals can be a centerpoint for the thrust of organizational effort. Their absence invites diffusion of this thrust, as individual groups create their own targets for lack of central leadership.

Goals and Goal Tradeoffs

As indicated earlier, goals occur in a hierarchy with the overall

29

organizational goals dominant. Setting of overall goals is a top management task. Then lower-level units in the organization can each develop an appropriate statement of potential contribution to the mission of the enterprise, and its own set of goals as its share in achieving the overall goals.

Simple as this process may seem, a carefully conceived set of goals is not easy to achieve, and even harder to apply to specific formulation of strategy. The difficulty is that often goals conflict, one with another. Tradeoffs and reconciliations amongst them are frequently necessary. A recurrent question is why some business planning processes do not yield better results. Often the fault is with poorly chosen goals or poor use of the goal structure.

"Tell me what your goals are, and I will help you to make a plan." This phrase is used so much by consultants and planning staff that it is sometimes called the planner's refrain. But if the manager does not really know what his goals are, or does not understand the implications of the goals that have been selected, planning effort will largely be wasted. A well-designed planning process will avoid this waste, and get a full measure of value-added from the planning effort.

The planning process often starts with cookbook planning. That is, the introduction to planning techniques is often, and properly, presented in the form of a series of sequential steps. The group is directed to proceed from one step to the next, and thus to produce a plan. This approach is necessary, but not sufficient.

The cookbook approach is only a starting point. Like the author of a cookbook, the experienced practitioner soon learns how to reinforce the process or deviate from it in order to get the best results. This is frequently necessary in planning, and the fallacy in the simple cookbook approach is the implied assumption that the steps in the planning process can be performed in a definitive way, one at a time.

That is, if the sequence is to go from mission to goals to strategy, and then to the details of the plan, the cookbook premise would suggest that these are independent, sequential steps to be completed in order. It would suggest that the "what is my business?" component of the mission analysis can be performed, goals determined within the framework of that mission, strategy aimed at the achievement of those goals, and so forth.

Unrecognized Assumptions

Of course, this simple sequential process represents a very desirable way to proceed, but the difficulty arises from unrecognized assumptions about the later steps in the planning process which are implicit in the selection of mission and goals. These assumptions often later require that the goals be adjusted or redefined, when they come to light. This requirement may emerge in cases involving hidden goals, goals with unrecognized and unacceptable consequences, and problems of conflict between goals.

HIDDEN GOALS. In one corporation the general manager of a growing but still marginal division was charged with building his business to a more satisfactory size and profit level. The desired rate of growth could only be achieved through acquisition. His plans spelled this out clearly, and they were approved by his superiors. But as he attempted to acquire suitable companies, he encountered road blocks and frustration. Again and again attractive acquisition candidates failed to win approval from his superiors, often for reasons that seemed trivial. Diligently he proceeded to bring in still more candidates, but with the same results. After several years of frustration he left for a better job with another company.

The flaw in the planning process, which finally came to light somewhat by accident, was that the senior executive to which this general manager reported had a fascination for businesses with a very high return on sales. Even though this executive had approved the goals and strategy of the divisional plans, this level of return had apparently become an additional yardstick against which he was measuring all potential acquisitions. This yardstick was probably not being applied consciously, for it was never clearly linked with the reasons for his rejections. And since there were no good acquisition candidates in this particular business area with a return on sales high enough to meet this hidden goal, it doomed the acquisition process to failure.

The planning process in that corporation did not focus on goals sufficiently to bring to light this conflict between the written goals of the general manager and the perhaps subconscious goals of his superior. Hidden goals which conflict so radically with explicit goals may be rare, but it is not unusual that different executives have their own personal views of the goal structure. These personal positions can diverge significantly if the planning process does not cause them to be explored and reconciled, and any such divergences will be built into the programs they administer.

GOALS WITH UNACCEPTABLE CONSEQUENCES. In another corporation the management agreed strongly on the necessity of diversification and on the need for an acquisition strategy to accomplish it. But as attractive candidates were brought forward, none were found to be acceptable. Finally, it emerged that these rejections grew out of an unrecognized goal to keep the present organization pattern and management style intact: "You never told us that if we were going to diversify we would have to change."

The group had made a commitment to a diversification goal without considering all of the consequences, in this case from necessary changes that new activities bring. In instinctive reaction against these consequences the management had defeated all attempts to pursue its own diversification goal. When this issue finally came into the open, management accepted the inevitability of some change and the program finally began to move forward.

As in this case, goals are frequently set without a full exploration of the consequences of pursuing and attaining them. It is not unusual that such exploration will either cause the goal to be modified, or another goal changed so that it no longer blocks the route to the desired achievement.

GOAL CONFLICT. A third type of goal problem is simple conflict between goals. For instance, profit and market share goals frequently conflict. Or in the public sector, inflation and unemployment goals conflict. Goal conflict can often be resolved by tradeoff, and where a simple choice between goals is possible, this is the proper course. Sometimes the goal conflict problem is more fundamental, and this will be discussed further after some aspects of the goal-setting process have been examined.

Establishing Goals

Management often defines its goals by getting together and talking about them. Generally the broadest goals are the easiest to set. The "motherhood, prosperity, and love of country" level of goals can be set down almost immediately, but this level of definition accomplishes little. While general goals are necessary and desirable as a beginning, they are so lofty and remote that they do not focus energy on specific programs and accomplishments. For goals to be useful they must be made specific enough so that the organization can act on them. As goals become more concrete and useful, they often become more difficult to define.

The purpose of having goals at all is to direct energy. The power of a good set of goals for mobilizing and focusing the energy of a large organization is as immense as the frustration when goals are left vague and different parts of the organization work at cross purposes without knowing which one is more nearly right. Thus the investment in management time to define a series of specific and actionable goals is many times repaid by the results.

Some goals lie beneath the surface and are rarely articulated. For example, many organizations act on goals related to the corporate style and personality and goals related to executive habits and self-interest. Since no management group is completely universal in its talents and qualities, it must set some limitations on what it will attempt. These limitations are often set by reinforcing the types of activities where the organization has the greatest experience and success and where the greatest interest for the executive group may lie.

To the extent that they aid a given management in making the best use of the available resources, these personal and organizational values are legitimate parts of the goal structure. Often the only practical expression of such limits is through definition of corporate style and characterization of the organizational culture. But such definitions and characterizations are rarely written down. Thus, specific action proposals may encounter goal barriers not perceived in advance because they were not clearly recognized or communicated.

How Detailed Can Goals Be?

There is also a limitation on the degree to which goals can be spelled out in advance, rather then evolving as decisions are made. While it is necessary that they be sufficiently specific and detailed to serve their purpose in focusing and directing energy, the goals should be kept as simple and brief as practical, with acceptance of the fact that instances will arise which the goals do not cover specifically.

Such an instance occurred several years ago when the managements of two chemical companies were meeting for the final agreement on the acquisition of the smaller by the larger company. For no obvious reason the negotiations were moving very slowly. After a time the large-company negotiating team called for a recess, and several members of the team visited the rest room.

On the rest room wall the senior executive saw a small sign proclaiming that one of the smaller company's products was in use there. He saw the difficulty: "Now I know what has been bothering me. I never want to find the name of my company on a rest room wall with the grafitti." He went back, expressed his regrets to the executives of the smaller company, and ended the acquisition discussions. The potential association between his company and a rest room product had violated a goal boundary.

In retrospect, this boundary was reasonably obvious, but while his company's goals defined chemical specialities business as desirable, the exclusion of this specific area had not been anticipated in advance. As in this case, specific issues often arise which were not foreseen when the goals were drafted, and it would be an undue burden on management time to attempt to detail goals sufficiently to anticipate every eventuality.

Goal Tradeoffs

The third of the goal problems listed earlier was that of conflicts between goals. Goal conflicts invoke a goal tradeoff process, as illustrated by the public policy issues concerning inflation and unemployment. While most public figures would prefer no inflation and no unemployment, most have adjusted to the hope of bringing both of these evils back to the level considered achievable in the past: therefore, common goals include bringing the inflation rate down to 5% and unemployment down to 4%. Even at these more realistic levels the goals still conflict and a tradeoff process is necessary.

This kind of goal tradeoff cannot be done on a once and forever basis because this would compromise the goals. Important basic goals are seldom compromised, although they are subject to a political process of negotiation between alternative practical actions — to choose the present action which fits the general goals best, no matter how bad the fit may be.

Thus, several times labor leaders have supported legislation which would not achieve major progress towards either the inflation or unemployment goals simply because such legislation seemed to be the best possible at that moment. Immediately thereafter the same labor leaders were again bending their energies towards other actions aimed at real progress towards less inflation and less unemployment. They had accepted the necessity of a specific immediate action without compromising their ultimate goals.

In dealing with goal conflict either at the national level or in the framing of a business plan, it is necessary to recognize these two goal levels. The first is a general level of goals intrinsic to the value system and essentially beyond compromise. Reduction of inflation and unemployment are good examples of such general goals. At the second level are the expedients which result from negotiation of the best means to advance towards the general goals at the moment.

These expedient steps represent compromises which must be negotiated over and over at every point of decision. They do represent goal tradeoffs, but not tradeoffs which can be defined in advance. Thus, a consumer who has a goal of buying meat at a particular price can hold firmly to the goal, but still buy angrily at a higher price as a momentary expedient, so long as this is preferable to not having meat at all. The importance of this distinction is that the acceptable tradeoff level is not predictable, so that it must emerge out of a specific negotiation process which an effective planning effort can catalyze.

Planning For Goals

To return to an earlier point in the analysis, the cookbook pattern of sequential planning usually does not work well unless the goal conflict issues are so minor that year-after-year plan recycles will have smoothed them out. Especially where important areas of conflicting goals must be negotiated during the planning process, this sequential approach fails, since it separates goal formulation from the definition of the action steps in the plan. Thus it often becomes important to keep the early steps of the planning process, particularly the goal definition step, sufficiently open so that it can be a part of the plan formulation process; a part which is tested for acceptability and restated as necessary as the plan is put together.

Properly directed, the planning process can be a major aid in goal formulation — whether the issue is one of finding hidden goals, helping management to understand the implications and consequences of the goals that it has already defined, or establishing the appropriate tradeoff level between conflicting goals. This planning for goals is an open process in which the implications and consequences of each step are balanced against the other elements in the plan to clarify the goals and define means to attain them. This should be a process in which the personality and style of the organization and the strengths and preferences of the individual executives are recognized in a legitimate framework and fitted together as a means to effective use of the resources of the business.

Planning for goals does not represent a change in the traditional planning process, except for the change in emphasis. By consciously keeping the goal structure open for reappraisal and refinement, more pointed and meaningful definition of alternatives becomes possible. Using today's array of management science tools, these alternatives can be characterized and contrasted by the appropriate staff. Multiple criteria decisions can be defined, and the interaction of various programs developed.

Decision analysis can aid in matching alternatives to the risk preferences of a given management. By getting the issues well clarified, useful analysis of management alternatives becomes possible. As the issues become clearer, management can better do its job. Complex national and multinational problems become more manageable, permitting timely, decisive action in any part of the world.

Progress Through Goals

The old planner's refrain should be restated, at least part of the time. Instead of "tell me what your goals are and I will help you to make a plan," it should become "let us design a planning process that will help you to verify your goals and then to achieve them." Then the effort can be better focused on the real planning problems, and is more likely to yield useful results.

The old concept of the retreat at which the management committee could define the goals of the organization and engrave them on two tablets of stone should be laid to rest. While it sometimes is necessary for a management group to get away and work out its aspirations and goals, it is equally necessary to recognize that the result of such a retreat is not a definitive product, because goal formulation is not a closed process. The better model is planning for goals as an open process, with modification of the goals as appropriate to build an optimum plan, and the objective of increasing the payoffs from planning through better management action.

Planning for goals is a part of the process of planning for action, since the payoffs of planning occur only when the effort is translated into management action. The goals are the basis for the action, so that the importance of the goal structure as an energy-focusing and directing force cannot be overemphasized. The choice between emphasizing a sound goal structure versus a more polished plan is somewhat like whether it is better to omit the engine or the fenders of an automobile. Without fenders the car may splash a lot. Without an engine there is no motion at all. In the same way the organization's goals catalyze forces for action, the most perfect plan is useless without action energy to drive it.

A well-managed planning effort contributes a value. This value-added contribution is the function which can be maximized by working to increase the efficiency and effectiveness of the planning effort. This means recognizing that the word 'planning' is an action verb, that planning can and should be a means to better management, and that planning for goals as a part of the process can be a means of getting more and better action as a result.

FOOTNOTES

[1]Portions of this chapter are adapted from George C. Sawyer, "The Hazards of Goal Conflict in Strategic Planning," **Managerial Planning**, May-June, 1980. p. 11-13, 27.

CHAPTER V

STRATEGY[1]

Given that a strategy is the necessary basis for achieving goals, its importance is obvious for any goal-oriented organization. While some firms have achieved significant profits very informally in the past, success without a systematic approach has become rarer as the business world has become more complex. A clearer understanding of what strategy is and how to formulate it is becoming increasingly important. Thus more and more managers are finding it necessary to learn the sequence of defining mission, goals and strategy, as well as how to turn the strategy into a plan.

A strategy is a road map to the goals; that is, an assembly of the elements which, when linked together effectively, permit a plan which moves the business towards the specific accomplishments it has chosen to attempt. But, what are the elements of a strategy, and what principles govern their effective linkage? What determines whether a strategy will be profitable? What are its several sources of profit? This chapter will look first at these elements individually, and then at the different sources of profit which condition the design of the resulting strategy.

Elements Of A Strategy

RESOURCES: One place to look for the elements of a strategy is in past successful accomplishments. Thomas Edison invented a light bulb and made it the basis for a major industry, initially supplying electricity for lighting homes, streets and businesses. Edison needed not only the light bulb he had invented, but also all of the other components of an electric lighting system — generators, switches, fuses, wire and electric distribution technology. To create, market and operate an electric system, Edison had to find capital, for the manufacturing and construction expenses and to finance the early period of operation before the business began to support itself.

In most businesses this pattern is repeated in one form or another. The product or service has certain unique features, it finds a need, and the entrepreneurial business musters the resources — that is, the financial, production, distribution, marketing, management and other components which permit it to be promoted, sold and delivered to the customer in sufficient volume so that the

37

business becomes self-sustaining. This sequence must be recognized in any list of elements of strategy, with assembly of resources as the necessary starting point.

DELIVERABLES: But resources, essential as they are, are only one starting point. The shaping of a strategy pivots around the definition of a customer need requiring satisfaction, and a deliverable product or service which will satisfy that need. Or, in the case of a strategy for an entire profit center, the deliverable must satisfy the needs towards which the operation of the profit center is focused. An effective strategy should be based on a need strong enough and a product or service good enough so that the deliverable can be considered as a pacifier for the recognized need. The best-conceived strategy is likely to fail, if the customer cannot be convinced of the importance of the need or that the product or service satisfies it.

DELIVERABLE: The product or service (or the catalog of related products or services) for which the strategy is designed, and which, in a cost-effective manner, must meet and satisfy important customer needs in the opinion of the customer; that is, the deliverable must be an effective pacifier for those needs.

RESOURCES: The necessary combination of technology, equipment, time, talent, money and positions required to implement a strategy successfully.

FOCUS: Consider an architect who after many years of training becomes expert in designing houses. That architect can work for U.S. Homes or another large manufacturer, or can go into the private practice of designing homes for individuals. Either route would represent effective utilization of the professional training. Both would be a part of the pattern of filling the customer need for housing, and would build on analogous patterns of resource utilization. But, in one case, the housing manufacturer offers a relatively standard product which the architect has designed, and sells it in a somewhat impersonal way. In the other case, to succeed the architect must become aware of the personality and life style of each client sufficiently to capture it in the design of the house. Just as with these two architects, businesses become involved with their customers' lives or businesses to a widely varying extent. This chosen degree of involvement also becomes one of the descriptors of business strategy.

Just as the architect and other professionals make career choices which define their degree of involvement with their customers, so do businesses that sell products and services. Different businesses choose to focus on different levels of need, and these differences in focus imply and require different resources for different market and customer services.

For example, a cosmetic company such as Revlon will promote to specific elements of its customer population, and may sell impersonally through drug and other retail stores. But when the sales effort is supported by a beauty consultant in a department store, a personal link to the customer is created as that customer is instructed in the use of the product.

The Avon lady carries this linkage farther. By coming into the customer's home, not once, but repeatedly, she has the opportunity not only to instruct the customer on the use of a product, but also to relate this to the customer's needs and lifestyle.

These are three effective ways to sell cosmetics, which reach different parts of the market in different ways and at different costs. Just as the architect could choose more than one mode of practicing his profession, the cosmetic company chooses to focus its efforts on a particular marketing channel and then assumes the role in relation to its customers which this choice of focus requires.

FOCUS: The defined relationship with the customers and the market place upon which a strategy is based. (Discussed further in Chapter XIV.)

LEVERAGES: This discussion has touched on some of the many sorts of resources a business must call upon to make a strategy work, and on some of the ways in which it can focus its efforts on a particular relationship with its customers. But why does the customer buy?

A customer chooses to exchange purchasing power for goods or services. The exchange is free and beneficial, even though the market may not be truly free. That is, the customer will only make the exchange if the perceived utility of the deliverable product or service is greater than that of the purchasing power which must be surrendered to obtain it. The marketer needs only to create and sustain the perception of value greater than cost in the customer's mind.

How then does a marketer create and sustain the perception of value greater than the price of a given good or service? In the first place, the product or service should possess this value, else the marketer is laid open to charges of misrepresentation and assailed by the sorts of ill will which make continued success unlikely. Given that the product or service must largely fulfill the claims made for it, the customer must be made aware of this value, and brought to perceive it in full measure.

Thus, a certain flamboyance and extravagance of statement is the mark of one sort of sales representative, and the advertising community is noted for the many and ingenious methods by which it seeks and holds consumer attention. This is a part of the art of leverages, to increase by all practical means the perceived stature and performance of the product or service, to create in the customer such an awareness of value that a purchase is likely to take place. To the list of strategic elements must be added those leverages by which the customer is induced to purchase that specific good or service.

LEVERAGES: The specific incentives to buy a given product or service, as perceived by the buyer; the reasons why the customer sees the deliverable product or service as a pacifier for specific needs.

POSITION: Henry Ford built from an effective automobile design by obtaining the resources necessary for production and marketing, and by creating the leverages necessary to cause the public to see the value. These marketing efforts, focused on a rather impersonal offering to a mass market through a variety of channels, brought success without precedent. Alfred Sloan, in recounting the evolution of General Motor's strategy, tells how Chevrolet found it impossible to compete head-to-head with Ford. A different strategic approach was necessary. Resources, leverages and focus can be used to explain Ford's initial success, but not why General Motors had problems in competing.

Chevrolet found it impossible to compete directly with Ford because Ford had built up a solid position in the market place. Because of his tremendous sales volume, Ford could manufacture and sell his black Model T at a price lower than any of the smaller-volume manufacturers, including Chevrolet, could match. This position had accumulated as a result of a consistently successful strategy which it then tended to perpetuate indefinitely. Again and again, in studying the performance of successful companies, it turns out that the positions they have built up over time are major resources contributing to their continued success.

In the Chevrolet case the solution was the used car. While a new Ford was the lowest-cost new-car purchase option available to a customer, in most cases his old car was still working well, and it was not easy to sell. Ford intended for Ford owners to drive his cars almost forever. But General Motors began to tell the customer all of the ways in which the Chevrolet was a better car — and to emphasize not the outright purchase cost, but the very small additional cost of a new Chevrolet when that customer traded in his old Ford. To make this process attractive, GM dealers worked hard to develop a market for the trading of used cars.

The appeal of the trade-in was a new marketing leverage. It encouraged the customer to trade up for a small additional cost to a new, better and more expensive car. This leverage appealed powerfully and Ford began to lose ground. Eventually the roles shifted, so that General Motors and Chevrolet had the established market position, and Ford was forced to strain to keep up. But only by inventing a powerful new leverage was General Motors able to successfully attack the established Ford position.

POSITION: Any consequence of past operations which can become a resource aiding in the design and implementation of new strategies. Valuable positions include those based on brand names and other market success, raw material costs or control, superior or protected processes and technology, cost advantages, and firm ties to customer need and habit patterns.

DISPLAY: Ford was only one of a great many early manufacturers of automobiles. Each of these entrepreneurs attempted to achieve leadership in the race to improve automobile performance, reliability and cost.

An early leader was the Stanley firm, whose steam car was probably better, safer and more reliable than the gasoline cars at that time. The Stanleys concentrated only on designing and building cars, however, and not on presenting them to the public. To buy a Stanley, one went to the factory and placed an order. Many people did this, and for some time the order backlog was substantial.

Ford and Chevrolet had started in the same way, but they discovered that the growth of their business was limited unless they arranged for display of the product. They began to establish dealerships, where the cars could be seen and ordered. Stanley never did this, and eventually faded from the scene, leaving unanswered the question of how much the steam car could have been perfected.

The choice of the desired degree of display of a product or service is an important element in design of a strategy. The customer must learn enough about the product or service to buy it, or there will be no sales. Arranging product or service display costs money, so that the strategic choice is the allocation of sufficient resources to obtain that degree of display consonant with the best overall results.

Some products sell themselves because the price or other features make them so attractive that buyers will seek them out, but these are the exception. Most products or services must be brought to the attention of the potential customer in some way, as people will see a display of flowers at a roadside stand and stop to buy. This process can be reinforced by advertising, to make potential customers aware that the product exists and where it may be found. Display can also be reinforced by demonstration, and the traditional role of the automobile dealer involves much demonstration and personal interaction with the customer.

Display sometimes overlaps with the other elements of strategy. The test drive and other elements of an automobile sale provide necessary display of the product and also give the dealer the opportunity to reinforce the leverages for purchase, and to focus at a personal level of interaction with the customer. In the same way advertising normally emphasizes the leverages at least as much as the display and availability of the product. But display stands as a separate element, requiring a separate decision as to the manner and degree to which a product or service must be displayed for optimum results.

> **DISPLAY:** The arrangements necessary so that potential customers can become aware of a product or service, and of how and where to buy it. Because it can bring additional interaction with the customer, display is often coordinated with focus, and with advertising of the leverages.

CASH FLOW: While resources, focus, leverage, positions, and display based on an effective deliverable are the primary elements, cash flow must be added to the list as a primary management control factor. All too frequently, particularly in the smaller enterprise, the management does everything else right — focuses on a customer need and builds the necessary relationship to promote an effective product or service deliverable, musters resources, designs and communicates leverages, and begins to sell, to grow, and to build a major position — only to collapse because cash runs out at a critical point.

Cash flow is one of the critical strategic elements because (I) unexpected cash shortage can handicap or destroy an enterprise, because (II) even where there is no shortage careful cash management is necessary to keep the investment in a given business or product within reasonable bounds, because (III) deviations from the planned cash requirements of a business are among the earliest and most sensitive indications of difficulties which may call for changes in tactics or strategy, and because (IV) the true commercial success of a venture is achieved only as cash flows back out to repay the investment and to yield an appropriate level of profit.

CASH FLOW: A progress measure and control element, to predict and track the implementation pattern of a strategy and to gauge its nearness and vulnerability to sudden failure or success.

Relating The Elements To Each Other

Resources, focus, leverage, positions, display and the definition of the deliverable — with control of cash flow, these are the key elements in any strategy, as summarized in Figure 1. They can be expanded — into a taxonomy of the major levels of customer needs which has proven useful in selecting a focus, for example. The interactions of these elements can be studied — such as the way in which the choice of a given focus changes a strategy's resource requirements, or the way that a shift from commodity to specialty product definitions brings new focus options and shifts resource needs.

This is a complex interactive system of seven variables, none of which are truly independent. If the product or its promotion can be altered to give it more of a specialty versus commodity appeal, it will be serving as a pacifier for a slightly different need, perhaps appealing to a smaller but more profitable market. Its strategy will require a different mix of resources, in part because the focus options change — specialty products often tend to involve a closer relationship with the customer and the details of his life or his business than commodities, and thus to require different sorts of product support. Also, specialty products tend both to offer and to need stronger leverages, to overturn buyer resistance and provoke a purchase decision. And, finally, while both specialty and commodity products can be the basis of important market positions, these are different sorts of positions requiring different efforts to build and with different sorts of value as resource components in future strategies.

Positions appear in the list of elements of a strategy first as a component of resources, and later as a separate element. In the short term a position established in the past can help very greatly in assuring the success of a new effort. And, if well managed, such a position builds on itself, as satisfied customers repurchase. The long-term art is to build the strongest and most durable positions day-by-day and year-by-year, and to merge them into a corporate

43

Figure V-1

Elements Of A Strategy

DELIVERABLE: The product or service (or the catalog of related products or services) for which the strategy is designed, and which, in a cost-effective manner, must meet and satisfy important customer needs in the opinion of the customer; that is, the deliverable must be an effective pacifier for these needs.

RESOURCES: The necessary combination of technology, equipment, time, talent, money and position required to implement a strategy successfully.

FOCUS: The defined relationship with the customers and the market place upon which a strategy is based.

LEVERAGES: The specific incentives to buy a given product or service, as perceived by the buyer; the reasons why the customer sees the deliverable product or service as a pacifier for specific needs.

POSITION: Any consequence of past operations which can become a resource aiding in the design and implementation of new strategies. Valuable positions include those based on brand names and other market success, raw material costs or control, superior or protected processes and technology, cost advantages, and firm ties to customer need and habit patterns.

DISPLAY: The arrangements necessary so that potential customers can become aware of a product or service, and of how and where to buy it. Because it can bring additional interaction with the customer, display is often coordinated with focus, and with advertising of the leverages.

CASH FLOW: A progress measure and control element, to predict and track the implementation pattern of a strategy and to gauge its nearness and vulnerability to sudden failure or success.

position of similar strength, because these entrenched positions contribute so greatly to success of future strategies.

The best short-term strategies are those which can take a proposed deliverable and select a focus, from the combination of potential leverages with an optimum redefinition or repositioning of the deliverable, and manage from the resources available to carry the product to market success. The best long-term strategies start where the short-termers leave off, weaving each element of the on-flowing business into stronger and better-buttressed positions. Where the short-term strategist must go back at the end of each product life cycle and search for a still-better new product, the strength of the long term position makes the products last longer and earn more profit, and makes easy the launch of successor products which need not always be so near to the cutting edge of new technology.

Some aspects of the management challenge of maintaining the ongoing success of an established company can be compared to rent-collecting — where the strength of the established position is so great that it earns handsomely just by its existence. Certainly the strategic requirements of continued success are vastly different than for an entrepreneur who must find market success without an established position to build on.

Combining The Elements

To return to the original question of what a strategy really is, and how managers can learn to define strategies successfully, the argument here is that understanding comes most quickly from a grasp of the elements of a strategy, and of their interrelationship and interdependence. A manager usually starts with a specific idea — for a new or existing product or service, or for a new business. Certain resources are available, including positions established in the past, or can become available if needed.

A focus must be chosen, where this is a commitment to a certain approach to the market place and to the market-support expenses which this entails, and sufficient leverages must be found so that the deliverable product or service can truly be displayed as a pacifier to a customer need. But usually the process of getting to this level of definition requires sharpening of the focus of the deliverable, and creative marketing research plus conceptual effort to build a strong array of leverages.

With all of these elements in hand the strategy is already partially converted into a plan; the planning process remains to be completed and the deliverable taken to market, where hopefully its success will be sufficient so that it will both generate profits in the short term, and contribute to the building of a position helping to insure the continuation of those profits in the future.

Sources Of Profit From A Strategy

Profit has many possible sources, and it is important in designing a strategy to understand what the sources of profit are upon which it depends. In his landmark work, *Theory Of Economic*

Development[2], Joseph Schumpeter argued that the only true profits are from innovation. He emphasized the importance of the innovation process and the economic and public benefits of its high early rewards. But an innovation never grows old; rather, it ceases to be an innovation, as others are attracted by the profits, enter, and compete the profits away.

When asked to explain the money earned and reported as profit from products not fitting his definition of innovations, Schumpeter pointed out that what is reported as profits often includes interest, rent, and other types of earnings.

For example, a broker or trader performs a service by making a certain type of transaction possible, and this is the basis for a trading profit. Or, a retail merchant or industrial distributor performs a service by financing, distributing and promoting merchandise so that it can be located and purchased by the final consumer. For this service the merchant is entitled to be paid, and the payment must compensate for the cost of the capital employed, including a proper allowance for risks in the transaction and a fee for the distribution service itself. Another type of profit would be the return to speculation or to gambling where the essential element is the skill or luck in playing against risk or uncertainty.

Where a high apparent profit level continues over a long time, Schumpeter's argument would lead to the conclusion that the nature of the money stream changes. If established initially as the return to innovation, this is a profit which will dwindle with time. For the same level of earnings to continue, other factors must begin to control. These other factors are those which describe an advantage in cost or access to customers, or barriers preventing the entry of competition.

The return which these other factors may properly earn is not an innovator's profit, but often a form of rent, as a payment to the owner for the use of the property. Rent was first defined as the return to the owner for its use of land. Ricardo's classic analysis of rent started with the return to tenants farming land of differing levels of fertility, where the poorest land from which crops could be sold for enough to cover the direct cost of production would continue to be farmed, but would earn no rent. Ricardo assumed the production costs on richer land to be identical, but the yields higher, with the difference in revenue from sale of the greater harvest representing the amount of rent the owner could demand for the opportunity to farm his rich land. Just as with land, other types of property and position can earn rent also.

The relevance of these distinctions to business and product strategy is that the money streams reported as profits in a modern business include other types of income earned in other ways. (See Figure 2.) In economic terms these reported profits are a mixture of true profits from innovation, fees for making a market and for distribution service, interest on the capital employed, and rents based on positions of ownership advantage in the marketplace.

While the stockholders generally will not care which source generates the stream reported as profits, management should notice and should care, because management of the positions generating each of these different sorts of money streams requires different strategies. When a product comes to market as an innovation and then continues to generate a return after the innovation has lost its newness, this has occurred because the management of the product has caused, or at least allowed, its continuation on the basis of different sources of profit.

Figure V-2

TYPES OF BUSINESS PROFIT(*)

Returns to innovation (The only true source of profit, according to Schumpeter).
Fees for distribution services.
Fees for brokerage service.
Interest on capital employed.
Insurance fees for business risks.
Gambling profits, where applicable.
Rents due to the differential productivity of resources employed in the business, or earned due to the strength of its established positions, including any monopoly.

*Profit as the net return from a particular business activity after applicable direct and allocated expenses and taxes.

Elements Of Strategy And Sources Of Profit

In fitting together the elements of a strategy, as summarized in Figure 1, with the sources of profit, as shown in Figure 2, some thought and consideration is necessary because of the way that the elements of a strategy overlap. Starting with leverages as the specifics encouraging purchase at a given price, the source of these leverages must be in the deliverable, and based either on the innovations which it represents or the positions which protect it, always recognizing that these positions are likely in their turn to be based at least in part on the other available resources.

47

To the extent that the leverages leading to the sale and resulting profit are from innovation, the profit is pure and proper, in the Schumpeterian sense. As other elements emerge also, other considerations enter.

General Foods has a valuable market franchise in the Jello product and trade name. No longer an innovation, the product is none-the-less believed to return an attractive profit. That profit includes a fee for distribution services — in that General Foods makes the Jello product widely and conveniently available — but where generic pudding products intended to serve the same customer need are available at one price, Jello commands a somewhat higher price. The difference is a profit of another sort — rent, in the economic sense — through a price premium earned by the strength of the franchise for Jello which good marketing of a good product has established over the years. And, if General Foods' cost of goods is lower than that of the generic competitors due to the higher production and distribution volume of Jello as an established, market-leading product, this cost difference represents another sort of rent earned by the production and distribution position, and adding to the total reported as profit.

In managing a product such as Jello, the nature of the different sources of profit are a proper part of the framework of the product strategy, and as these sources change with the evolution of the product life cycle, optimum product strategy will shift correspondingly.

When Librium was first marketed in 1963, it represented an important innovation, soon followed by the parallel but somewhat different innovation of Valium. These two products have utility as tranquilizers which was not possessed by predecessor products, and both seem to have a permanent place in tranquilizer therapy.

Both products are known to have been quite profitable for the innovating company which brought them to market, and the initial profits were clearly a return to innovation. But as these products have grown into maturity, the continuing profits are no longer innovator's profits.

Generic chlordiazepoxide, the Librium substance, has been available for several years at a fraction of the Librium price, but slow to penetrate the market because of the strength of the Librium franchise. Traditionally, the pharmaceutical products market is willing to pay a very high rent — again in the economic sense — to the holder of an established product franchise — in part because of continuing concerns about quality differences of generic products, and more because the doctors who prescribe the product find that it is easier to practice good medicine by keeping the drug, which is a small part of the cost of the treatment regime, constant, and varying other factors in search of better health response from the patient.

But not all of the pharmaceutical companies seem sensitive to the inevitable shift of a new product profit base from innovation, where Librium profits were initially derived, to rent based on different positions and franchises plus a distribution fee, as are now the basis for Librium profits. Failure to understand this shift could lead to imperfect product management.

More dramatic is the consistent short-fall of the recurrent activist and public sector attempts to establish generic prescription products as a means of cutting pharmaceutical company profits — where the cause of the failure is largely due to a fundamental misunderstanding of the nature of the franchise upon which the use of the higher-priced products depends. Had the drug companies and their opponents each developed clearer insights as to the nature of the profits they have been quarreling over, several companies might have fared better competitively, but also the generic prescription efforts could have gained market share faster.

The central point for all product and business management, starting with proper definition of product or business strategy, is to identify the different sources of profit on which a given product or business depends, and then to develop a strategy to make best use of this potential — using leverages based on the positions which earn each sort of actual or potential profit.

When Xerox launched its major early leasing program, it was choosing to sell a copy service on a per-copy basis rather than to sell copy machines. While the final consequence — making Xerox copies — was the same, the copy-service concept brought in another source of profit from the service, in addition to bypassing the customer problems over financing machinery capital costs.

Or, American Hospital Supply in its period of early growth removed a large part of the hospital supplies inventory risk from customer hospitals by guaranteeing quick delivery of a wide variety of items, so that the hospitals need not order until the product was actually required — thus the hospital could manage with minimal inventories. The distributor was paid for these services — but was better able to manage inventories and inventory risks than the hospitals, so that the consequent and continuing distribution pattern is both economically efficient and profitable.

In the same way insurance companies make a good business out of underwriting risks that they can manage more economically than client companies, and commodity speculators by their speculations permit the hedging of grain purchase prices — where this hedging allows producers to enter into contracts for future delivery of meat or processed foods which would otherwise be too hazardous.

The number of examples could be multiplied further, but the underlying point is already made: there are many sources of profit in commercial transactions, and innovation is only one of them, even though it may be the only 'pure' source in an economic sense, and the richest, long-term, in a commercial sense. Good strategy often involves using several sources of profit, but this diversity can only be managed effectively if the different profit elements are recognized both for their contribution to the positions and leverages upon which the sales volume depends, and for what each source of profit has cost to develop, since the resulting profits must eventually be measured on a return-on-investment basis.

Levels Of Strategy

Drucker speaks of the urgent management task of creating customers, and any business is founded on a customer need for products or services. Since customer needs in a market of some sort are the basis, strategy should relate to satisfaction of customer needs. However, these needs are addressed on three very different levels:

I. **PRODUCT STRATEGY** — and any functional strategies required to implement it — deal with achieving goals related to successful conception, development, production and marketing of specific goods or services.

II. **BUSINESS STRATEGY** — and any functional strategies required to implement it — deal with achieving a mission and goals related to the successful management of a business unit — the development of its markets, its line of products or services, its production positions and physical plant, and its relationships with other institutions and with society.

III. **RESOURCE STRATEGY** — and any functional strategies required to implement it — presume that management has proceeded successfully enough with product and business strategy to have alternatives between businesses; resource strategy deals with the allocation of the available resources between businesses.

The preceding discussion of the elements of strategy and sources of profit has been built on techniques for relating both products and businesses to the customer needs and markets which must be the foundation of any business. Resource strategy uses the same elements but combines them differently.

Thus a business management often must decide whether to integrate, either vertically or horizontally. Vertical integration forward towards the market or backward towards the raw materials is an additional use of resources to be evaluated on the basis of its contribution to the positions, leverages, and sources of profit of the business, versus its impact on cash flow and return on investment. Proposals for horizontal integration can be evaluated in the same way.

Diversification — the allocation of resources to other businesses — can be concentric, where the relatedness of the businesses may contribute to the positions or leverages of each and make the overall management task less difficult, or conglomerate, where high return-potentials are normally selected in spite of the negative impact on total corporate positions due to the increased difficulty of the overall management task.

The importance of these three different levels of strategy is to recognize that they exist, and that they require slightly different analysis of the same underlying situation. All three build upon the same strategic elements, but not in exactly the same way. In particular, errors are possible at the resource strategy level if various alternatives are not related to the underlying customer need and business situation upon which each potential use of resources is based.

Strategy And Its Alternatives

The purpose of determining what elements of strategy are available, and what sources of profit, is the definition of the best of many possible strategies for a specific business or product at that point in time. The process of searching for the best strategy should include definition and at least partial exploration of all major alternatives. However, too often a group will become enthusiastic over the first workable alternative which is uncovered, and never look further.

Chapter XIV will discuss techniques for evaluating strategic alternatives, but here it is important to emphasize that alternatives almost always exist. The first precaution against major strategic blunders is to recognize all of the major alternatives, and to understand enough about the implications and consequences of each so that the choice which is made will not be based on a false perception of the available options.

Any list of alternatives should be headed by the status quo. That is, in most situations one of the alternatives is to do nothing, to

51

continue exactly as before. Where this is truly not possible, this alternative can be excluded, but otherwise it should be in the list — in part because in very many cases the inability or unwillingness to make a difficult decision results in continuation of the status quo, even though this may be one of the poorest choices.

The alternatives should be listed, with care, and with an effort at completeness. It is important that this first listing be neutral and value-free. If the person making the list is allowed to color it with opinions, this tends to blur the evaluation exactly in the area where clarity is needed most.

Given a reasonably complete and value-free list of alternatives, the decision-makers should review the list and begin to exclude the poorer alternatives for specific reasons. But, again, the quality of the resulting decision is improved by the discipline of defining briefly why each alternative is discarded.

The result of the process will be a much shorter list — perhaps only one alternative, or perhaps two or three. In this way it should be possible to get rather quickly to the major choices which need to be made, but without blurring the evaluation process or hiding critical issues. Then the major alternatives can receive as much evaluation as may be necessary to refine the choice, so that the best strategy is finally selected.

However, the end result of the strategy selection process is often not truly an end result, because it can only reflect the best information and understanding at that moment in time. The basic circular and iterative nature of the planning process arises because as the process flows from stage to stage it brings new information and new insights, and often these will then require revision of some of the previous stages. Thus the evaluation of a given alternative, and its examination through the strategic modeling technique described in Chapter XIV, will often lead to a new understanding of its consequences, and bring the need to reexamine and redefine the original list of alternatives.

The optimum definition of strategy starts with a strategic overview and a thorough understanding of the issues and their background, and continues until a strategy has been selected, evaluated for its consequences, turned into a plan, and the plan has been reviewed and found truly to offer the desired progress towards accomplishment of mission and goals. By working from the available elements of strategy, combining them creatively, and selecting the best of the alternative courses of action, management's planning can make the maximum contribution towards the organization's progress.

FOOTNOTES

[1]George C. Sawyer, "Elements of a Strategy," **Managerial Planning,** May/June 1981, p. 3-5,9.
[2]Joseph Schumpeter, **Theory Of Economic Development**, Oxford Press, New York, 1961.

CHAPTER VI

THE STRATEGIC OVERVIEW[1]

In order to formulate strategy successfully, the different elements in the strategy must be interrelated. Managerial choice of one component of the strategy becomes a constraint requiring consistency of the other components, if the total strategy is to be effective. Perception of the relevance of each of the elements in the strategy and of the structure of their interrelationship requires a breadth of information and a depth of insight beyond that encouraged or permitted by effective management of day-to-day operations.

Operating managers often cannot formulate successful strategy. This chapter will consider the reasons for the normally limited perception — essentially a strategic blindness — of the otherwise competent operating executive, and the means by which a more adequate strategic perspective can be obtained.

Planning, Barriers, and Strategy

All managers plan. That is, all managers have an ability to lay out patterns of action in advance, else they could not function. This planning may be a personal, intuitive process, or even subconscious. And this type of planning often fails to fill the need of an organization that its managers plan together. It is not enough that each manager lays out his or her pattern of action in advance. These plans must be developed jointly, negotiated, shared and communicated, in order for the pattern of action-laid-out-in-advance efficiently to move the organization in the direction dictated by its overall strategy. Many barriers within the organization hinder the movement from individual to shared planning.

Additionally, the manager inside of an organization is unlikely to have all of the necessary information for effective planning. This means that these information needs must be anticipated and filled, most often by the planning function, if the shared planning of the line managers is to be truly effective.

The most frequent barriers to planning in the large organization are (I) walls erected by line managers who have not learned how to share plans, (II) the failure of line management to achieve a perspective of the organization and its problems from which valid strategic choices can be made, (III) the need to anticipate the information needs for planning and have the information at hand, and

(IV) inefficiencies due to the spontaneous degeneration of the organization. The failure to see where the organization is going can be the most catastrophic, but degradation of the organization can have equally serious impact over time.

Spontaneous degeneration can be rapid if an organization is being managed without positive pressure for improvement and without a valid perspective of the problems and the opportunities from which valid strategic choices can be made.

The problem in achieving an adequate perspective is the consequence of the concentration which any good manager develops and applies. Concentration is a focusing of attention. It is achieved by excluding extraneous information, and admitting into conscious perception only that information related to the problem at hand. To permit concentration, the conscious mind is protected by a series of barriers which can be set to minimize or exclude penetration of undesired signals. Some teenagers can study effectively in front of the television because they have the ability to block out the sound, and to concentrate on the task at hand.

Managers individually set barriers admitting some types of information and excluding the rest, as do their organizations. Each executive secretary has a series of criteria determining which incoming messages reach the executives to whom they are addressed, and which are shunted aside to be handled by others. This screening is a part of the exclusion process required for concentration, but it necessarily causes a narrowing of the point of view of the executives working within such barriers.

Rather than examining each component of the total environment each time that it relates to an operating matter, the members of an organization tend to use simplifying assumptions based on past experience, or to depend on information summaries supplied by others. Between the individual and personal concentration barriers and the information screens and filters of the organization, a management group isolates itself from interference very effectively.

It also isolates itself from new trends in the outside world. While this screening out of stray information is a necessary part of an efficient operating pattern, it leaves such an executive group with an insufficient perspective of the total flow of events to deal successfully with formulation of corporate strategy. This is the condition defined here as strategic blindness.

While the executive group concentrates on effective current operation, protected by its screen of concentration barriers, the larger aspects of the day-to-day function of the organization tend to be left to natural processes. The organization, as an open system of interrelated individuals, tends rapidly to develop a life force and a biological identity of its own, and to strive to continue and to protect this identity. As Stafford Beer once put it, "An organization is an institution dedicated to being what it is, and doing what it does."[2]

The organization was brought to life as a system linking people and operations. It attempts to perpetuate itself and to fulfill its given purpose by protecting itself against change. It organizes each task more and more completely, details more exactly the nature and purpose of each linkage, and makes each procedure more comprehensive and elaborate.

In the attempt to pursue its given purpose the organizational forces will, like Mary Shelley's Frankenstein, transcend and attenuate the efforts of their creators if unchecked. The cure is through management as each element of the organization and of its procedures is examined, evaluated, and freshly adjusted to the most effective operating pattern.

In an organization where management has not established a strategic overview perspective its need to manage the organizational system itself is often not obvious. Individual managers concentrating on effective performance of individual assignments tend not to detect a change, as the overall organizational system deteriorates under the increasing weight of its organizational processes.

Since the perceptual barriers defined above are a normal result of effective operating management, the problem of how operating executives can overcome strategic blindness in order to formulate strategy successfully is one which almost every organization needs to solve.

The Strategic Overview

The need is to establish a strategic overview of the business, its customers, its suppliers, its industry and its environment, as a condition of effective strategy formulation. This means accepting, considering and evaluating much of the information normally rejected by the concentration barriers of the individual managers in the organization, to see whether it is becoming a part of any pattern relevant to present or future strategic needs or plans.

Since such evaluation is itself a violation of habits of concentration validated by operating experience, executives not already skilled in strategy formulation rarely understand this need. Either by adding a separate cadre of management charged with responsibility for corporate strategy, or by causing the executive group occasionally to withdraw from operations sufficiently to assume a different point of view, a strategic overview must be achieved before

56

the attempt to formulate strategy has reasonable prospects of success.

This shift of viewpoint is not intrinsically difficult, but requires a conscious effort and some training. It will probably not be successfully achieved except by an executive group that fully understands the necessity for temporarily shedding the security blanket of its familiar operating viewpoint.

The purpose of achieving a strategic overview can be expressed in terms of the management requirements of the five dimensions of social impact, opportunity, course correction, operations, and self-renewal, as pictured in Figure 1. These, together with provision for gathering the necessary information for planning, comprise strategic overview management:

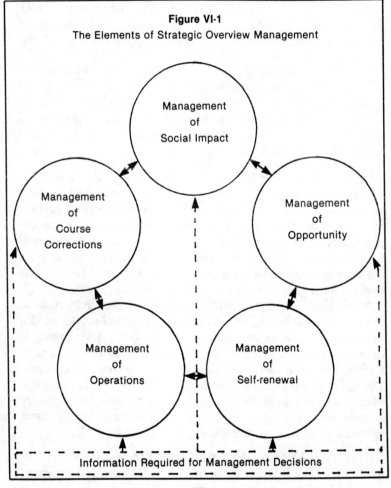

Figure VI-1
The Elements of Strategic Overview Management

Management of Social Impact

Management of Course Corrections

Management of Opportunity

Management of Operations

Management of Self-renewal

Information Required for Management Decisions

(1) THE MANAGEMENT OF CORPORATE SOCIAL IM-PACT. A corporation and the surrounding society have an interdependent, symbiotic relationship, to the extent that almost any major activity of one affects the other. Just as a big fish in shallow water causes the water to churn with every movement, so does society react to the impact of corporate decisions. Where the public once accepted these impacts as a necessary part of progress, today's society questions them more and more.

Where corporate social impacts have come to public issue, regulations have usually resulted. Thus, railroad abuse of the powers inherent in a service monopoly led to curtailment of management's freedom of action through the creation of the Interstate Commerce Commission. Similarly the Consumer Product Safety Commission, the Occupational Safety and Health Act and various activities of the Environmental Protection Agency each represent regulation which reduces corporate freedom to operate in response to public concern over real or apparent abuse of this freedom.

The corporation can ill afford direct confrontations with society. Major corporate energies are diverted by such confrontations, and society normally prevails in the long run anyway. Thus, corporate self-interest calls more and more strongly for the anticipation and management of the social impact of corporate actions, to reduce the chance that such a confrontation will arise.

(2) THE MANAGEMENT OF CORPORATE OPPORTUNI-TY. Not only do products have life cycles, but markets develop, mature and change. Industries and technologies become obsolete; others replace them. The concentration barriers around current operations normally restrict management horizons to today's products and new products like them. While the R&D function often can develop new products on demand, the welfare of the business requires more than replacing yesterday's products.

A failure to consider the wider horizons will eventually result in attenuation of growth, senescence and even decline, as market characteristics change and margins narrow with market maturity. In the long run, resources must be shifted from market area to market area, in order to sustain corporate existence and growth. This is the function of the management of corporate opportunity, which assures that the financial and managerial investment pattern is designed to be consistent with realistic and continuing routes toward achieving corporate goals.

(3) THE MANAGEMENT OF CORPORATE COURSE COR-RECTION. The continual flow of new requirements, new restrictions and new liabilities from outside of the corporation offers a continual hazard that major programs will be disrupted by elements which are non-strategic or even trivial, just because they happen to be the subject of a new regulation. Thus, when a food color is banned or a chemical additive is found to cause cancer, ongoing programs are halted as abruptly as when a car or truck breaks an axle in a pothole. The need is to look ahead and steer around such obstacles so that corporate strategy can proceed unimpeded.

Thus, Graham Molitor[3] reported that General Mills, warned by him of impending regulatory problems, removed red dye #4 from its products before the actual ban came. While its competitors got unfavorable publicity and were forced to reformulate in the heat of the moment, General Mills' programs proceeded undisturbed because it had steered a course around this particular obstacle. This is an example of a corporate course correction. The need is to anticipate and avoid such obstacles on as systematic a basis as possible.

(4) THE MANAGEMENT OF CORPORATE OPERATIONS. This is the demanding and difficult job of keeping the daily operation running smoothly. Planning, organizing, staffing, directing and controlling are elements of operations management, and each has its strategic components which change with changing external requirements. In addition the operating system is normally expected to absorb and adjust to most social and technological change without disruption or loss of efficiency. This requires good managers and a clear overview of the relevance and futurity of today's problems.

(5) THE MANAGEMENT OF SELF-RENEWAL. While a corporation may be eternal in its legal form, too often in actuality it is as mortal as its first successful products or its first president. For an organization to go on through time it must have a successful pattern for replacing its managers, and for adjusting and streamlining its own operations in the face of the spontaneous degradation processes described earlier. This is the process of organizational self-renewal. This process is a critical management task and requires a strategic overview perspective for its adequate performance.

These are the five dimensions of strategic overview management. To overcome the normal strategic blindness of operating management, plans are needed for these five dimensions, together with the means of gathering necessary planning information in advance of the moment of need.

Strategic Overview Management

The concept of strategic overview management is based on an effective concentration on management of corporate operations, the essential day-by-day function that pays wages and makes the profits. At the same time and from an adequately detached viewpoint, plans are considered for the management of: social impact, opportunity, course correction, operations themselves, and self-renewal, so that, day by day, energy can be kept focused on those areas most strategic to the continued success as well as the continued existence of the firm.

Each of the five dimensions of strategic overview management will be discussed individually in subsequent chapters, as will the information-gathering process necessary to anticipate and meet the needs of analysis, planning and management of these five dimensions.

FOOTNOTES

[1]Adapted and expanded from George C. Sawyer, "The Use Of Strategic Models In Setting Goals, *MSU Business Topics,* August 1979, pp. 37-44.
[2]Stafford Beer, International Conference on Corporate Planning, Montreal, December 8-10, 1971.
[3]Graham Molitor, "The Process of Socio-Political Innovation," Industrial Management Center Conference; Castine, Maine, June 16, 1976.

CHAPTER VII

THE MANAGEMENT OF CORPORATE
SOCIAL IMPACT

Management of the relationship between the business and the various elements of the society around it has become one of the major tasks of corporate executives. A major objective of this management task is to maintain a maximum degree of freedom to operate in an increasingly difficult political climate. The route towards this objective starts with the handling of today's confrontations, litigations, and crises, and extends to building a better external relationship in hopes of a less turbulent future.

The essence is that the business corporation is a part of society and totally dependent upon it. Society, as the dominant political force and the rule-maker, must at least passively accept the pattern in which the business wishes to operate. Society sometimes seems to forget that it depends on the business corporation to give employment and to produce the goods and services society needs and that profit is required if the business is to continue to exist.

This relationship is a kind of symbiosis, like a marriage where neither partner can live without the other. The only question is whether corporation and society will share pleasure or pain, since they cannot survive separately.

The original source of the strain between corporation and society was in abuses of society by its business enterprises as industry developed. Most of these abuses — at least we view them as abuses today — were both legal and socially acceptable at the time, but this has been forgotten. Society has discovered that it suffered in the past through pollution, injury to workers, dangerous products, waste of resources, and in other ways, and has become angry. Individual firms and the business community as a whole are now viewed with deep suspicion, to the point that many elements of the public gleefully harass large corporations whenever the opportunity presents itself, and seek ways to obstruct corporate projects.

Each business needs to develop and maintain a viable relationship with society in the face of these attitudes. At the same time it needs to work to overcome and redirect that momentum from the past which dominates many organizations. This inertia of past actions is of two types. First, much existing industrial plant was designed and built to meet standards now obsolete. Violations of today's requirements were once viewed as sound designs for facilities still seemingly too young for abandonment, but not now protecting workers or the public adequately by our new standards.

In the second place many managers learned their own standards of how a corporation behaves in society long ago, and times have changed. In many cases they still give yesterday's answers to today's questions, and are only slowly moving to full understanding and acceptance of society's requirements. Many corporations have compounded their difficulties with society by responding to criticism from a position grounded on obsolete and irrelevant standards.

Most major corporate decisions impact society significantly in one way or another, and society has become highly sensitive to these impacts. Confrontations with regulators and the public are increasingly frequent and expensive, absorb massive amounts of management time, and usually result in concessions to society's wishes.

Given that each business wants a maximum degree of freedom to operate in pursuit of profits, corporate self-interest requires that the executive group anticipate and manage the social impact of its actions, to avoid unnecessary or unintentional confrontations with society. Therefore, a key component of strategic management in any profit-seeking corporation is a plan for the management of corporate social impact, and a key element of a strategic overview is to obtain a clear enough perception of social forces and stresses to design and manage such a plan successfully.

This chapter will summarize the elements of a plan for managing corporate social impact, drawing material from George C. Sawyer, **BUSINESS AND SOCIETY: MANAGING CORPORATE SOCIAL IMPACT**[1] , where the subject is discussed in greater detail.

Managing Social Impact

The concept of managing the social impact of corporate actions is based on three fundamentals:

(I) There is an overall benefit to society from sound operation of the business.

(II) Society will require on behalf of its individual members that losses or injuries resulting from corporate actions in any specific area of operation be at least balanced by positive actions or other compensation in the same area.

(III) The social impact of corporate actions and the reactions of society can largely be predicted. A management will benefit significantly from looking ahead, estimating the probable impact of actions not yet taken, and redesigning these actions if they have unexpectedly adverse impacts or risk unnecessary confrontation with society.

The operation of any profitable business is normally beneficial to society because it is making and selling goods or services worth more than their price to the purchasers. In each case the buyer voluntarily surrenders purchasing power, whether in money or credit, in exchange for the good or service. The transaction would not occur unless the purchaser valued the good or service more highly than the purchasing power which was exchanged. Since each individual purchase benefits the buyer, in his or her own eyes, at the moment of purchase, the total effect of all of the purchases of goods and services from the firm benefits the purchasers as a group and society as a whole.

There are only two reasons why society would not benefit from the operation of a profitable business: (I) If the products or services sold by the business do not meet the expectation of the purchaser at the moment of purchase — due to fraud, misrepresentation, injury or side-effects to the users, faulty design, and so forth, or (II) if the business has not paid the costs of its operation, since its profits are the difference between the revenues received from the purchasers and the costs it pays.

Good business ethics and several laws require that the purchaser of a good or service should actually receive the value that is represented to be in the product at the time of purchase, and that that purchaser be able to use the product without untoward effects. By and large, therefore, business plans and performance should be based on giving the purchaser the value invoked by the seller to win the purchase decision.

The costs of a business operation are more difficult fully to judge. While a business will pay for its labor, raw materials and supplies in the normal manner, this may not fully compensate the costs of the operation. Pollution, for example, results if more waste is discharged into a stream by a business than the natural systems can manage. Society is injured by the damage to the stream, and the business has avoided paying a waste treatment cost.

When society must support disabled workers, the costs resulting from dangerous working conditions are being left for society to pay. One of the past failures of both business and society was fully to understand what the costs of a business operation really are. In the absence of this understanding such costs often were not fully paid.

A business should fully and fairly pay its costs before it calculates and claims profits. This requirement is fair but not easy, because some of the cost calculations are difficult.

The costs of pollution are often large and hard to quantify, but the costs of waste treatment to avoid the pollution are much less, easier to measure, and represent the solution society desires anyway. The costs of the various sorts of adverse impacts of corporate actions on employees, customers and community are often equally difficult to quantify, but many can be avoided by alternative actions in the same way that treating waste avoids the social costs caused by dumping untreated waste.

The total wealth of a society is called the social capital — where this is the sum of the physical and natural resources of the area and the skill and training of the people.[2] Social costs caused by a business and left unpaid reduce the social capital. The requirements for a corporation attempting to pay its costs is to operate in such a way that in each area of its operation it does not reduce the social capital.

In returning to the three fundamentals underlying the plan for the management of corporate social impact, the first, that the operation of the business is basically beneficial to society, is fulfilled if the goods and services meet the prepurchase representations and if the business fully pays its costs, where this second requirement is clear but not always easy to fulfill.

The portion of the requirement for fully paying costs which says that the injuries to individuals in each area of operation be compensated is equivalent to the requirement that any adverse social impact in that area be balanced. Although a business cannot always trace out the full effect of its decisions on various members of the community, for example, it can attempt to keep the net effect on the community positive, as is easy for a business giving steady employment to do.

The third fundamental was the generalization that, by looking ahead, management, or its staffs, can usually foretell its impact on society as a result of a given action, and often can estimate the intensity of the reaction an adverse impact will produce. Even though this prediction process is imperfect, the potential for avoiding the delay, cost and drain on management time of confrontation with a public interest group, regulatory agency, or other instrument of society makes the forecasting and management of corporate social impact well worth the effort.

For purpose of the management of social impact, the universe of corporate actions has been divided into eleven areas, five where the major impact tends to be mostly local, and six areas where the impact spreads more generally across the social system. Specific guidelines are suggested for management action based on this analysis of these eleven areas.

Direct Impact Of Corporate Actions

CONSEQUENCES OF THE SALE OF GOODS AND SERVICES. This area deals with the issues which arise after a sale, all related to whether the purchaser received value as represented. The considerations include (I) the requirements for adequate after-sale support of some types of products, including parts and service where the customer could normally expect such support, (II) an adequate standard of product safety, including recognition of safety hazards to others, or through normal types of misuse, (III) recognition of the effect of the product on life styles; e.g., the consequences of the famous advertising campaign which helped make it respectable for women to smoke, thus doubling the cigarette market and the number of people exposed to the alleged risk of lung cancer, and (IV) the environmental consequences; e.g., the aluminum soft-drink can, and the issue over litter by the roadside; or, the fluorocarbon aerosols and issues over damage to the upper atmosphere.

A strong corollary incentive for careful design and control of products and services is the rapid rate at which the risk of product liability and other types of legal judgments is increasing the financial exposure of businesses which leave themselves open to complaints over the quality or safety of the things they sell.

USE AND CONSUMPTION OF PHYSICAL RESOURCES. In the course of its business an enterprise uses some resources without consuming them; an example would be the land on which the corporate headquarters is built. The business also consumes different sorts of resources according to its nature. While the firm purchases these resources and obtains a property-owner's right to use them, society has an increasingly acute interest in destruction or depletion of scarce resources, whether sequoia forests and oil reserves or farm land paved for shopping centers. Strip mining continues as a center of controversy because of the environmental effects of the mining, and several mineral and petroleum exploration projects have been blocked by similar issues. Thus it becomes important to consider the local and national social implications of scarce resources as a part of a business's plan for continuing to use them, preferably without governmental interference.

PEOPLE AS RESOURCES. People are a consumable resource of the business — each individual has about 10,000 days in his or her working life, and as this time span passes by must manage career, family and personal aspirations within boundaries set by wages, working conditions, opportunities for advancement, and provision for dependents and for the later years. Hazardous materials and bad working conditions cause people's working lives to be used up faster than by the normal aging process, and such injuries have caused strong social reaction — ranging from the workmen's compensation laws and the national black lung program for coal miners, to the developing spectre of corporate liability for injuries such as cancer from exposure to asbestos. Less dramatic, but almost equally important, is the judgment that the corporation is liable for chronic conditions — such as noise in the workplace which may have caused a worker's hearing to decay at greater than the normal aging rate.

The management burden in the human resources area is to use people with care, with a respect for the dependence on the business which normal employment practices encourage, and still to require effective and efficient performance. This requires design of meaningful work, of potential career paths such that personal ambitions need not conflict with personal goals, and a style of management leadership which both encourages and demands willing performance.

WASTE FROM THE BUSINESS OPERATION. Waste from the business operation should not harm the environment, whether the pollution is from liquids, solids, gases, noises or heat. In attempting to work to acceptable pollution standards it is necessary to recognize three different types of treatment problems: (1) biological waste; that is, human, animal and vegetable waste which can easily be digested by conventional treatment plants, (2) toxic wastes, such as cyanides, which require extreme dilution and special conditions but can then be handled by conventional treatment processes, and (3) system-level poisons, such as mercury, DDT, PCB's, and other materials which may not even show their potential toxicity in the initial treatment, but concentrate and persist in the environment.

New system-level poisons are being discovered every year, and any corporation needs to be alert to potential liability from discovery that past discharges have contained a system level poison; e.g., the continued expense to General Electric because the mud of the upper Hudson River is poisoned with PCB's even though GE had obtained explicit permission to discharge this material, which was then believed to be harmless.

The preceding discussion of liquid wastes applies also to discharges into the air wherever injury can result or residues, such as lead or arsenic, may be deposited in the region. Solid wastes are a special problem, because (I) they fill dumps, and dumps tend to be a permanent use of land, a scarce resource, and because (II) old chemical dumps are yielding unpleasant surprises every year. Considering the way in which dump contents tend to outlast the public attitude and regulatory climate in which they were established, and the potential liability many years later, it has become an unwise financial gamble to put unknown or toxic material in any dump — e.g., Hooker's nightmare with the Love Canal. It appears far wiser to arrange final disposition of the material on a current basis, so that it can never be resurrected.

IMPACT OF THE FIRM ON THE LOCAL COMMUNITY. Business and community are interdependent, and support each other best when both are in good health. A business and its employees are substantial users of community services and substantial supporters of them also through the business' own taxes and those derived indirectly from its payroll through the employee group. Therefore, business has a strong self-interest in a well-run, efficient community with services adequate for its employees, and also an interest in helping the community to plan efficient and effective services to the non-working portion of the community based on its share of the financial contribution.

System Wide Impact Of Corporate Action

Society depends on continuing business operations — in part, to manage well enough so that the business grows, providing continuing and increasing employment and economic vitality in the region, and so that the business itself represents a growing component of the social capital. This makes the corporate asset reallocation decisions more difficult, because of the problems in attempting to cushion shifts such as withdrawal from an area.

BUSINESS AND TECHNOLOGY. Each business has its own need for technology — for its own innovations to strengthen its product or service sales position, or for the innovations by others to be applied to strengthen operations and increase productivity. Many important innovations are new applications of scientific knowledge in combination with existing resources. The pool of fundamental scientific knowledge is limited, although it expands as basic research continues in university, government and industrial laboratories. Any technology-dependent business working near the frontiers of scientific knowledge has a need to concern itself with whether fundamental work is being done at a rate which will support continued new product development.

BUSINESS INVOLVEMENT IN PUBLIC ISSUES. More and more, all major business decisions are actual or potential public issues, because of the social impact of these decisions and the desire of society to control such impacts. Therefore, any significant business has a permanent role in public issues which concern it. Further, businesses are often used as an instrument of public policy, in dealings with other nations, for example. In their turn firms ask for public policy support at critical times; e.g., the Chrysler request for loan guarantees. Business also becomes an active participant in government processes, testifying for congressional committees, advocating public or legislative action, and seeking regulatory approvals of many different types.

MEETING AND SHAPING THE REQUIREMENTS OF SOCIETY. Business has a profound impact on community culture, from the cumulative impact of its advertising, the way that its ethical and moral standards of conduct spread through the community, and its interrelationship with the development of the society. Because of this key role the tendency therefore is to require slightly higher standards of conduct from businesses and business leaders than from the average citizen. And, when business behavior has failed to meet public expectations, new regulations and agencies have sprung up to regulate its conduct more tightly.

GOVERNANCE OF AN INDUSTRIAL SOCIETY. The corporation is the wealth-producer in today's society. Living standards depend upon how fast wealth is manufactured, and how many people must share it. As our society has devoted more and more of its wealth to social overhead, in the form of big government and expanded social services, this has meant that a smaller fraction of the population must produce the wealth. So far, their productivity has risen faster than the demands on them, and average living standards have increased — but this continuing increase is now in doubt.

The broad national problem is how an increasingly complex industrial society can govern itself, and how a more efficient and effective system can be devised to accomplish increasingly complex regulatory tasks at an affordable cost. The most effective and efficient system requires a maximum of private sector activity, with strong economic incentives and penalties to insure that the system functions according to the public will.

CORPORATE LOYALTIES AND ALLEGIANCES. As corporations grow across national boundaries, the logic of their operation needs review. Since they need both corporate charter and social approval in each political jurisdiction, it follows that local subsidiaries must seek to blend in and become a part of the local society, in order to be acceptable in the long run. This also means that the subsidiary must look first to the interests of the society of which it is a part, and second to the interest of its parent. This leads to a pattern of multinational management of a federation of partially autonomous subsidiaries where the subsidiary's loyalty must be first to the local society. Similarly each corporate employee can be expected to look first to his or her own career path, and the challenge to the employer is to make a parallel between these interests and the interests of the corporation.

Guidelines For Management Action

In order for a management to maintain a social balance, so that the impact of its actions will not disturb a profitable relationship with society, it is suggested that the following guidelines for management action should be observed:

MERCHANDISE QUALITY. On the whole, goods and services fulfill the expectations of the purchasers.

SERVICE. Reasonable requirements for after-sale product support plus continued support of routine use patterns are met.

SAFETY. Goods and services are free of danger and unexpected side effects in normal use, attempt to insure the safety of predictable types of product misuse, and do not cause unacceptable environmental aftereffects directly or from their packaging.

IMPACT OF NEW PRODUCTS. When goods and services that change life styles and cultural patterns are introduced and promoted, an effort is made to minimize disruption and resentment, and, thus, to avoid future challenges from society concerning the right to introduce such goods or services.

CONSERVATION. A firm whose operation is using or consuming scarce resources develops an understanding of the role of these resources in the total social capital, both in actuality and in popular belief, and manages its operations with a sensitivity that minimizes the chance that its right to use these resources will be restricted or withdrawn.

VALUE GIVEN AND RECEIVED. Each member of the organization receives fair compensation (including adequate provision for dependents and for old age benefits), works under conditions that do not impair health now or in the future, and in return is expected to deliver full productive energy during the time allocated to the job.

OPPORTUNITY. Meaningful tasks, challenging career paths, and equality of opportunity to pursue these tasks and paths are maintained with minimum possible disruption.

POLLUTION. Wastes discharged from the business operation do not cause any measurable detriment to the environment.

BUILDING DUMPS. Wastes going to land fill or ocean dumps or otherwise making permanent use of the earth's surface area require appropriate social consent for this dedication of land or ocean resource; nevertheless, such discharges are best minimized or avoided in anticipation of increased dumping costs and restrictions.

RESOURCE WASTE. Energy and resource content of waste streams are minimized by recovery or recycling as an operating economy; this also provides a means of reducing environmental burdens in anticipation of further social pressure toward more careful resource use.

DEPENDENCE. A firm recognizes the degree to which it is dependent on and served by the health of its surrounding community and encourages this health wherever and however possible.

FAIR SHARE. A firm operates in such a way that it and its employees support their fair share of the costs of community services, including those used by the business and needed both by the employees and the fringe of the community.

NEIGHBORHOOD EFFECTS. A firm recognizes its own effect on the nature and character of the neighborhood around the operation and minimizes adverse effects insofar as possible.

MAINTENANCE OF CAPITAL. A business operates to conserve and expand its resources in order to maintain and increase the level of opportunity in its own interests and in the interests of its employees and the dependent community.

USE OF PROFITS. A business handles its profits in such a way as to minimize the economic, social and political impact of their use, particularly the impact from any movement of profits from the business to a parent corporation or to the stockholders.

ALTERNATIVES TO SEVERANCE. When evolution of the business creates a surplus of plants, people, or community services, the firm makes a serious attempt to find alternative, profitable uses for these dependent resources, or at least to cushion the severance so that the long-term economic health of former members of the organization and the health of the community will be preserved.

TECHNOLOGY. A business dependent on the long-term processes for generation of new technology develops an understanding of this dependence and seeks opportunities to encourage replenishment of this technology.

IMPACT OF DISCOVERIES. A business engaged in offering goods or services based on new technology recognizes the responsibilities, which are growing but are still imperfectly defined, for the consequences of the social impacts that derive from the right to introduce new discoveries.

PUBLIC SELF-INTEREST. In public processes a firm recognizes and pursues its own self-interest as it relates to the social and political processes in such a way that neither the anger of society nor its political power will be aroused.

RESPECT FOR LAW. A corporation obeys the law and cultivates respect for it from others.

SOCIAL CHANGE. The corporate power to mold and reshape society subtly is used wisely, by selecting areas where the social forces justifying and supporting the change have already been set in motion and by not encouraging any change that will cause a major clamor for rejection by society's governance processes.

WEALTH PRODUCTION. As a wealth producer, and in the interest both of its own economic soundness and that of society, a firm attempts to make its productive processes as efficient in the use of materials, energy, and labor as competitive circumstances will permit.

REGULATION. As a regulated wealth producer, a firm strives to build public information about and awareness of the basic issues underlying the choice of the most efficient pattern for regulating it and its industry. Thus, necessary debates over alternative governance processes can more likely lead to wise political and economic decisions.

ALLEGIANCE. A corporation gives its primary allegiance to the society that makes the rules controlling its existence. In the view of that society, it must blend in as a sound corporate citizen to have hopes of long-term acceptance and survival.

FEDERAL MANAGEMENT. A corporation with operations in many different nations or other rule-making social units encourages each subsidiary to become a part of the local society. Then the corporation must manage its affairs through a pattern of corporate governance that recognizes the divergent allegiances of the several subsidiaries and develops economic and managerial unity within a framework consistent with these local ties.

POWER. A corporation uses its economic power and its political influence with great circumspection and discretion to avoid presenting threats to the society or confronting the political power that controls the corporate existence.

EMPLOYEE LOYALTY. A corporation expects and requires allegiance from the members of its organization within the scope of these employees' normal growth and progression as individuals. The corporation also recognizes the likelihood of unrest and defection if it should attempt to require illegal or unethical actions or actions detrimental to an employee's own self-interest.

Self-Interest And The Management Of Corporate Social Impact.

The preceding guidelines for management action focuses on the maintenance of a smooth relationship with society. This includes fully paying its costs as it operates in society, which also gives the resulting profits a new legitimacy. As developed earlier, a business which is treating its customers fairly and fully paying its costs benefits society by its operation. This benefit does not depend on the profit level — the business is free to make as much profit as it can. Once all costs are paid, Adam Smith's invisible hand of competition and self-interest serves society's interests very well. Businesses should work as hard as they can to sell more and make more profit, and society will be better off as a result.

Of course, some businesses are not able to pay all of their costs. At the conventional accounting level the eventual solution is bankruptcy, if a firm cannot pay its costs. When only the social costs remain unpaid, the issue is different, as when the federal government had to decide how rapidly to enforce coal mine safety regulations in Appalachia a few years ago. Here the choice was between allowing a continued excessive rate of death and injury to the miners, or demanding expenditures which would force many marginal mines to close. These mines were operating without paying the social cost of their impact on the miners — and depleting the social capital of the region through the shortening of productive lives and the increase in the welfare burden. As in this case, society must decide whether to subsidize a marginal business by allowing it to draw on the social capital in order to keep operating, or to force it to shut down.

Where Did Social Responsibility Go?

Does business have a social responsibility?
Of course it does, but what is it?

72

The problem with the social responsibility concept is the extreme difficulty of definition and management — because it involves social concepts incompatible with the economic fabric of a business enterprise.

The approach suggested in this chapter is a simpler one, because it is possible to treat customers fairly, and at least to approximate and balance any adverse impacts of the business on society. Once these impacts are balanced, meaning that all social and other costs are paid, the corporation is free to pursue profit in exactly the way in which its economic nature and purpose dictate.

Thus, the social responsibility issue is both acknowledged and bypassed — with its burdens sufficiently discharged by fair treatment of customers and full payment of cost so that the business can concentrate on the benefit to society it then renders by whole-hearted pursuit of profit. The plan for the management of corporate social impact, advocated here as a key component of strategic overview management, is intended to aid the business in achieving a social balance and the resulting operating freedom which it brings.

FOOTNOTES

[1]For an expanded discussion see George C. Sawyer, *Business and Society: Managing Corporate Social Impact,* Houghton-Mifflin, Boston, 1979.
[2]Sawyer, OP. CIT., pp. 118-120.

CHAPTER VIII

THE MANAGEMENT OF OPPORTUNITY

Business and industries always have had their cycles of evolution and maturity, and these cycles move faster now. But for a management walled off by its concentration barriers in an ivory-colored tower, today's crises are so demanding that the slower shifts of the underlying business often go unnoticed. The aging of markets and the emergence of new opportunities pass undetected, because a positive effort is required to keep the organization's energy properly focused. That is, a positive effort is required to track and manage opportunity, the subject of this chapter.

Three Opportunity Programs

The strategic overview requirement is for a perception which can be developed into a plan for managing opportunity that contains three programs. The first is a program for keeping the present businesses smoothly attuned to their shifting and maturing markets.

The second is a program for aiming R&D at future markets. This is to insure that the products which replace today's products will be geared to the market in which they emerge. A market often changes in the time between definition of an R&D target and the marketing of the product or service which which this research produces. The risk is that, if there is not a conscious effort to look ahead, tomorrow's discoveries could be geared to yesterday's markets, and the products obsolete before discovery.

The third program is, as necessary, to shift resources to new areas, to avoid being boxed in by the boundaries of the present markets and to find growth areas as needed.

Any management should decide how much it needs or wants to grow, and the plan containing these three programs should be designed to accomplish this growth. The amount of growth a given management group may wish to attempt depends on many things including the individual ambitions of key executives, but there are also sound operating reasons for seeking growth. To make the corporation easier to manage, it is suggested that the growth goals should call for a growth rate (I) which will minimize the effort required to maintain an acceptable social impact level on the community and (II) which will make it easier to provide the necessary personal opportunities for the members of the organization. In a growing organization a positive social balance with the community is easier to maintain, promotions and new job challenges come faster, and top management can more easily establish and maintain that congruence between personal and corporate growth and personal reward paths that characterize the most dynamic and effective management groups.

To assemble a plan for management of corporate opportunity requires an insight into the nature of the product and business life cycles, the next subject. Then the discussion will return to the central concept of an opportunity-discovery-and-development process and of the tools for its management.

Product Life Cycles

Products have life cycles. New products become old, and may be replaced by newer products. The markets for these products expand, contract or change in other ways as the product demand is affected by economic and social variables.

Product life cycles are of many types; Figures 1 and 2 show two of the extremes. Figure 1 is a life cycle typical of a capital goods item with a fixed total market, or of a consumer product which is almost totally replaced by a better product or a newer fashion. The product is brought to market as an innovation, goes through a period of evaluation and testing, wins market acceptance and begins to sell rapidly. As its potential market begins to saturate, sales first peak and then fall to a replacement level, which may be too low for the product to stay in the market. Or, when a product is replaced by a better product, this cuts off the expansion of the market and causes sales to fall.

Figure 2 shows a product life cycle which starts in the same way, but differs in that the product finds a permanent place in the market. As it matures, the sales shift from a growth curve to some other curve governed by variables affecting demand in its markets. This life cycle might be typical of a commodity such as table salt, polyethylene or vitamin C, or a consumer product such as Listerine or Jello which wins and holds a market franchise over a long period of time.

These two life cycles are defined in simple terms, and many intermediate forms exist, as well as subtleties such as the effects of changes in promotional support or modifications of the product. However, these simple cycles provide the basis for suggesting that the optimum strategy for any particular business is very much related to the sort of products and expected product life cycles on

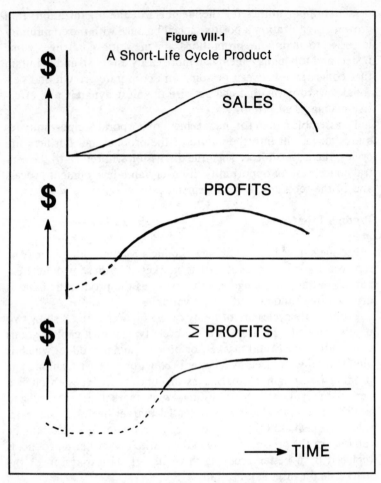

Figure VIII-1
A Short-Life Cycle Product

which that business is based, and to tactics which may serve to modify and extend these product life cycles where appropriate.

A business which is based on short-lived capital products such as new instruments, or on one-time service projects such as the construction of a plant or the successful completion of an R&D project, determines its size and growth characteristics largely by the size and effectiveness of the development effort which attempts to bring in new products or projects faster than the old ones are completed or fade away. On the other hand as a business with long-lived products grows, the management will be increasingly more concerned about how to maintain acceptable profit margins as a larger and larger fraction of sales come from mature products in the later phases of their development — and therefore this management will tend to be relatively less interested in new products.

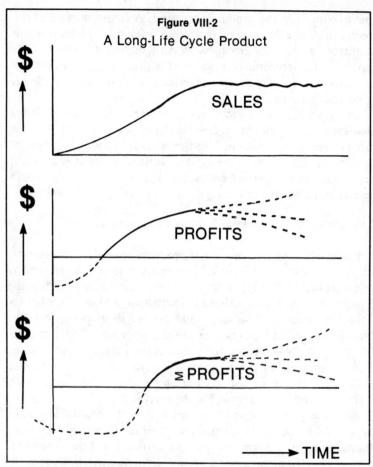

Figure VIII-2
A Long-Life Cycle Product

SALES

PROFITS

≤ PROFITS

TIME

In both Figure 1 and Figure 2 the profit curves show initial losses, with a breakthrough into profitability at some point early in the rapid growth of sales. The curve for the summation of profits correspondingly reflects the before-marketing and after-marketing investments as losses, with start of repayment as the product becomes profitable, breakeven as the product approaches maturity, and finally the start of return to the investment.

The short-product-life business must be a high innovation business, in that it must develop new products or sell new projects at least as fast as the old ones fade away if it wishes to exist over the long term. Such product or project development is normally a significant expense, and an important fraction of the resources of such a firm tends to be devoted to this activity. While the products or projects which result need to be profitable on a current basis, it is even more important that, on the average, these profits exceed the investment in the product or project. A frequent cause of difficulty in such a business is the failure of a series of individually profitable projects or products to earn sufficient profit fully to repay the development costs, so that the firm consumes an element of its capital as each successive new activity moves through its life cycle and fades away.

The business with long-life-cycle products has different challenges and problems. Initially each product passes through the same stages of development investment, early losses and repayment through profits. Then as the product matures it assumes different profit and market characteristics, and the product strategy should change to reflect the changing basis for its competitive strengths.

Life Cycles and Businesses; Portfolio Management

Businesses are based on sale of products or services. Businesses, as stated earlier, also have life cycles. A research department is often created to find replacement products, and success moves the business beyond the limitations of individual product life. Markets have life cycles also, however, and as they develop they tend to mature and to change in nature and characteristics. These changes often are in the direction of lower margins, greater competition, and a lower rate of major product innovations. Often there is a shift from a market evolution guided by creative sellers, to one with a stronger and stronger role for the careful buyer.

New and fast-growing businesses tend to be profitable but to have high investment requirements. Often the cash flow burden of financing growth in an exciting new market is a heavy one, and high-growth companies are traditionally cash-poor in their early years. The reason that deficit financing in these years is widely practiced is that, as the products and markets begin to mature, investment requirements usually diminish and cash can flow back out of the business to repay the investment and provide a return. Several major corporations have based a major part of their approach to corporate strategy on the recognition that the different businesses in a diverse corporation tend to be at different stages in these cycles, and need to be managed quite differently if they are to yield the desired level of return over that cycle.

In one such system the new businesses start at the NASCENT stage, move into an INVEST-GROW phase, then into a MATURE phase, and finally into a DIVEST/WITHDRAW phase. In the first two phases they normally represent a cash drain. Even though the invest/grow stage is normally one of high profit margins, current asset requirements grow rapidly with the business, and good development of the overall potential requires high fixed asset investment often.

During the mature phase investment requirements normally drop, profits continue, and the business generates cash which can begin to repay the investment and fund new ventures. Then as the stage of maturity advances, profits begin to fall and the future of the business becomes less and less attractive. At some point the harvest/divest stage is reached, where the management attention shifts more and more to recovery of as much of the invested capital as possible, whether by liquidation or divestment.

These stages are real, recognizable, and useful in managing the businesses. However, a given stage has no fixed time span, so that one business may stay in the same stage of development for many years while another moves to the later stages rapidly.

The stages-of-growth type of analysis described above can help to gauge where in such a portfolio of businesses money should and should not be invested. At the level of corporate resource allocation the payoff from analysis of alternative strategies for the many businesses in a diverse corporation is a superior decision on where to invest. Where part of the emphasis is on finding the best possible strategy for a specific business at a specific time, the other emphasis is on comparative tools to gauge whether a business merits investment at all, or should be sold or liquidated. The relative weight given to these two approaches depends on the point of view of the business' manager versus that of the investor.

The analysis defined above is one of several parallel patterns. General Electric, Arthur D. Little, the Boston Consulting Group, and Westinghouse have published similar categorizations. These are valuable tools, because they help to emphasize the necessary shifts in business and investment management from stage to stage. Where rapid investment in an invest-grow business is normal and its absence suggests mismanagement, a mature business normally requires little additional capital, and the reasons for any significant investment should be examined with care.

General Electric also requires that each of its businesses define the growth of its markets as high, medium or low, with the general intent of concentrating investments on fast-growing markets and of moving out of declining ones, unless unusual features of a specific business militate otherwise.[2]

Another interesting tool is PIMS, a comparative profitability system also developed for GE under the direction of Sidney Schoeffler, who now manages this as an independent effort.[3] By compiling and compositing confidential financial data for specific lines of business as supplied by subscribing companies, average data is produced; this gives the subscribers a yardstick for comparison with their own performance data. PIMS is now widely used, particularly in the longer-established and more mature business sectors.

The purpose of the various stages of business growth measures, the measures of market growth, the PIMS comparison with other similar businesses, and several other types of comparative tools is as an aid to what is often termed a portfolio approach to strategic management of a complex business enterprise. The concept is that since the business normally consists of a wide variety of distinct business units — GE defines separate strategic business units as the basis for its planning — the management style should recognize this diversity, and use it as the basis for investment and divestment decisions, thus shifting its portfolio of businesses in the direction of maximum opportunity for growth and profit. The consequence of this portfolio approach can be to move resources from one business area to another, and thus to accomplish the third of the three programs in the plan for management of corporate opportunity.

Opportunity Management

Successful management of corporate opportunity requires a plan containing three programs. These are the programs for (1) changing today's business, (2) replacing today's products or services, and (3) changing today's investment areas. These are not changes for change's sake. These are calculated, necessary changes to keep the corporation and its businesses at least abreast of the change processes operating around it, and to provide a reasonable prospect for sustainable growth.

The program for changing today's business operates from external information on the change processes in today's markets, and from time to time will signal the painful need to abandon a trusted product or technique which is no longer relevant.

The program for replacing today's products draws on both the conventional and the creative wisdom of the R&D unit, and uses the same external market change intelligence to fight against the eternal technical desire to perfect solutions to present problems no longer relevant in the projected future. Neither Research nor Marketing will be entirely comfortable with even small deviations from the present market reality, and the necessary prediction of the future is uncertain at best. This is a most difficult program to manage, because the R&D group must be brought to focus on the world as the management group comes to believe that it will be when the product gets there.

The program for changing today's investment areas drives off of the other two, as well as from the external information about the markets. To the extent that programs (1) and (2) give the necessary and desired pattern of growth, changes in investment area are not necessary — but management can only judge this after reviewing the opportunity spectrum based on the best available information.

Management of corporate opportunity requires handling a demanding package of programs, but this is not difficult for able managers with a clear perception of shifting external and internal variables. It requires a strategic overview perspective because effective management of corporate opportunity would be impossible if management's protective barriers to perception of external relationships were not first lowered sufficiently to permit this planning.

FOOTNOTES

[1] Joseph Schumpeter, *Theory Of Economic Development,* Oxford Press, New York, 1961.

[2] William E. Rothschild, *Putting It All Together,* Amacom, New York, 1976, Chapter 8.

[3] PIMS services are offered by the Strategic Planning Institute, 955 Massachusetts Ave., Cambridge, Massachusetts 02138.

CHAPTER IX

THE MANAGEMENT OF CORPORATE
COURSE CORRECTION

Corporate course correction is a steering concept, and the plan for its management is a plan for steering the enterprise so that it will remain on the course defined by its goals and strategy.

In steering a vehicle, an enterprise, or any other moving body, there are at least two components — a direction, as defined for a business by goals and strategy, and the frequent small adjustments to local conditions necessary in order actually to follow the preselected course. One comparison is with the steering of a ship, where the rudder setting is almost continually adjusted to compensate for wind and ocean currents which otherwise would cause the ship to drift off of its course. Another example is the challenge of driving a car on an unpaved country road — where the driver must actively steer from moment to moment, in order to pick the smoothest course, to dodge rocks and holes, and to stay on the road successfully.

The Plan For Course Correction

The plan for corporate course correction is a plan for the sort of short-term expedient changes of direction dictated by conditions of the moment. Its scope is the entire universe of non-strategic variables, appropriately narrowed to those specific trends and events which could potentially impede or divert the corporate direction and thrust, if timely corrective action were not planned and executed. The plan for corporate course correction requires a strategic overview because it deals so much with incidental impact of otherwise unrelated programs and events which would normally be blocked out by management's concentration barriers.

One biological products business which had thought itself totally unaffected by the 1973 OPEC oil embargo suddenly was unable to buy acetone, a solvent required for its production processes. Operations were interrupted and sales were lost. Over the years acetone, once made from corn, had become a petrochemical — because low-cost petroleum fractions provided a cheaper raw material. Adjustments were easily made to use alternative solvents and the interruption lasted only a few weeks — but because this management had not recognized the shift to dependence on petrochemicals, the business was caught unprepared.

What The Plan Includes

Not all such dependencies can be anticipated and avoided, but most of them arise only slowly and their impact is predictable, given a sufficient overview and the necessary information. To try to avoid such incidental derailments of business operations, the plan for corporate course correction focuses on the interrelationship between the stream of events in the society around the business and (I) the resources the business requires for its operation, (II) the processes and procedures by which the business operates, and (III) the manner in which that firm's goods or services reach the customer and are purchased.

In analyzing these three dimensions, there are other considerations, including changes in regulation, changes in availability, and changes in social/institutional control. Changes in regulation are frequent and pervasive in their impact. In the example cited earlier, when the FDA banned food use of the color Red #4, this was a change in regulation which made a specific color unavailable to food companies — that product could no longer be purchased and used. General Mills, forewarned of the ban, had made an easy adjustment to other colors. Other companies found the need to withdraw and reformulate products, to their own embarrassment in the market place and with some loss of sales.

The Occupational Safety and Health Administration (OSHA) has introduced many new regulations intended to make working conditions better. When OSHA put strict new controls on vinyl chloride vapors, this required vinyl plastic fabricators to choose between shutting down and rebuilding almost completely with new fume control and air purification equipment. While the new standards were a great financial shock, their arrival was foreshadowed by laboratory reports of cancer in animals, public discussion, and a rule-making procedure in which industry groups had the opportunity to participate before the regulations became final. The point is that the arrival of an expensive new standard did not need to be a surprise; interested firms which had an active function fulfilling the corporate course correction role knew the general nature of the proposed new standards for a considerable period of time before they had to begin to comply.

Changes in availability of resources are more often anticipated by the operating processes of a business than the other changes in the corporate course correction area. But even here there are surprises — as the companies using silver for industrial purposes found when the price suddenly rose more than ten-fold. Yet while the specific price rise at that time perhaps could not have been predicted, the general conditions favoring a sharp rise in silver prices were clear to many analysts, and the fact of a large rise should not have been a surprise to any interested corporation which was looking ahead systematically.

These examples deal with physical resources, but human resource shortages are equally subject to anticipation and adjustment. The classic story is that of the Bell system requirement for telephone operators for the original manual switchboard network, which threatened to limit the growth of the system. It then was projected that the need for operators would grow to exceed the national supply of women who then constituted the potential labor force. This projection was said to be one of the key elements in the justification for the long term and successful investment in the development of automatic dialing equipment. Similarly other corporations have used their own projected need for technicians, programmers, or specific professional qualifications as the basis for planning training programs and liason arrangements with those schools turning out the proper kind and caliber of graduates.

The need for corporate course correction also arises in the market itself. New requirements are placed — by building codes, new purchasing procedures, or new concepts of consumer protection. Explosives which once were freely available for purchase now are restricted to channels where there is a legitimate industrial or construction use. Suppliers who formerly sold to certain governmental agencies can no longer do so unless they establish that they are in compliance with current affirmative action and equal employment opportunity statutes.

Another major source of necessary corporate course corrections relates to events in the surrounding political and social climate. Dow Chemical management felt that it had a duty to continue to supply the Defense Department requirement for napalm during the Vietnam War when other suppliers dropped out, and seemed not to have anticipated the extent of the public reaction. Dow gained relatively little by this, as this was a small element of their business, and not especially profitable. But Dow became the focus of antiwar protest, to the point that Dow recruiters were forced to curtail college campus visits, and boycotts hurt sales of some Dow products.

Businesses doing business in South Africa have had similar political fallout adverse to their business. Local issues have caused even sharper confrontations — a few years ago supermarkets and other retail firms doing business in inner city areas found themselves the target of well-organized boycotts which forced heavy hiring of blacks and minorities — not because these businesses had been slow to integrate, but because they were the most convenient and accessible targets of the aroused wrath of that community.

How To Steer The Ship

The way that a corporation avoids most of these pitfalls is by looking ahead, planning action, and steering the corporate programs around these obstacles as well as may be possible.

THE FORESIGHT FUNCTION. The looking ahead requires a foresight function — a function or separate staff that searches for external trends with potential relevance to the business, gathers information on the relevant trends it finds, and presents for line management consideration a timely package of information, analysis, and alternative courses of action. This function must have very broad information horizons, as will be discussed further in Chapter XII, and an understanding of the way in which change occurs in today's society.

Changes rarely or never occur abruptly or without a supporting context. The challenge to the foresight group is to define the relevant context, learn to read its evolution, and then to anticipate and suggest changes which will avoid adverse impacts on corporate programs as external changes occur. This is done from the point of view of the plan for corporate course correction being discussed here, but the actual work of a foresight function is much broader, as it supplies information related to all of the strategic overview components and to market and technology management also.

An example of change and its context can be drawn from the recent turbulence in Iran. While the specific events of the Iranian revolution could hardly have been predicted, the growing social stress within the country was known and noted by many observers, and the U.S. government has been widely criticized for not taking more seriously the signs that serious trouble was approaching. Now, with Iran as a model of the problem, a number of consulting services are offering projections of the political stability or instability of various countries as a potential service to multinational corporate clients.

This is foresight-type activity — and in corporations where political instability of small countries was relevant to the planning, the foresight function would have included this dimension. But inside the U.S. the issues tend more to be the trends in regulation, social legislation, tax reform, and so forth — or the extent to which trends towards new and different life styles and personal value systems will continue to change consumer markets. While each of these areas is a special study in itself, there is a broad pattern to

85

change, with incubation, discussion, agitation, lobbying — growing interest, stress, and controversy — and finally a change, if the process fully matures.

HOW IT WORKS. New ideas emerge first at society's fringes — perhaps art and science fiction show the earliest indications. Then articles begin to appear in magazines at the borders of political or social respectability, or which specifically cater to new events. Many new developments in medicine are first reported in **Lancet**, the British journal, and many scientific developments have first been reported in **Science** because both strive to provide a forum for important new developments.

Such an early report has no immediate business relevance, except as an element which can later become a part of a pattern. The foresight function concerns itself with such scattered and potentially relevant items and watches to see if the pattern will develop. A new political theory, a campaign to establish national health insurance, or any other such event starts with weak and scattered signals, and then is picked up and amplified as it gains support. In the case of national health insurance, after several years of building support, the issue reached major stature on the national political scene and several groups which do foresight-type analysis first predicted its adoption by Congress during the Johnson administration. The evidence was a combination of a political trend towards this type of health care which had started in Europe — developments in the U.S. often follow patterns set in Scandinavia, but 10-15 years later — the desire of Senator Kennedy and several other political leaders to use this program as a platform, and a judgment of the general support in Congress and in the country.

National Health Insurance has not yet become law, and as an issue it has at least temporarily receded from the political scene. However, it serves to illustrate the general problem and the general approach — where any corporation with business interest potentially affected by a national health insurance plan has real interest in closely monitoring the development of the issue.

Another type of change where foresight groups claim success is in predicting regulatory activity. The prediction of the banning of Red #4 as a food color was cited earlier, and is a good example. Here there was a context of regulatory trouble for the chemical family to which this dye belongs — several chemical cousins had been proven to cause cancer in laboratory animals and had been banned. That Red #4 would be subjected to the same tests was obvious, given the announced Food and Drug Administration programs, and the first tests showed the potential that this dye might be proven dangerous. Most chemicals which have encountered these initial doubts have failed later examinations and been banned, and there was no commanding health or economic reason why Red #4 would survive if not cleared of suspicion. An astute forecaster saw this pattern and warned his employer that the color should be replaced. This was not difficult to do, and the color was removed from the company's products well before the ban came. This is the way that a foresight group is supposed to help with the plan for corporate course correction.

To restate: a foresight function looks for patterns that experience has shown are likely to precede a particular event. If the pattern is seen, the possibility of the event is reported and recommendations made that this possibility be considered in planning. The pattern will show stress or political pressure, or economic strain, but not the specific event. Just as the stress preceding the fall of the Shah of Iran was or should have been evident, or the probability of a world oil crisis in the early to mid 1970s was predicted, a political momentum sufficient to pass a national health insurance bill was measured and reported. The background work from a foresight function can be excellent and an invaluable aid to planning, but the prediction is based on stress and momentum, and often does not foresee the specific event.

The purpose of a foresight function is to help to look ahead, to alert Planning and line management, so that issues needing decision can be anticipated and decided in a timely way. Particularly for the corporate course correction plan this function or some equivalent source of the same sort of information is important to effective planning.

The Course Correction Concept

The heart of the entire concept of a plan for corporate course correction is in the concept itself. Once a management has understood the need for specific consideration of the class of social, political and economic variables that the plan for corporate course correction deals with, and once it has delegated the necessary foresight activity, the planning and implementation of the course correction activity blends back smoothly into the strategic planning process.

Corporate course correction needs to be sufficiently separate to be sure that it does not get forgotten — but is an easy extension of the other planning activities once the importance of the concept of anticipating and avoiding obstacles to corporate programs becomes clearly understood by management.

CHAPTER X

THE MANAGEMENT OF CORPORATE OPERATIONS

As a component of strategic overview management, the plan for the management of corporate operations deals with the structure and strategy of those operations, and with the guidance necessary to cause them to evolve in an orderly way.

The norm of any operating system left to itself is for it to assume a strong self-direction, to become increasingly rigid in its procedures, and to be totally resistant to change. While many of the characteristics of this norm are desirable and help to keep a well-planned operation running smoothly, the system rapidly becomes obsolete if a constructive and evolutionary pattern of change is not planned and directed by top management.

The Management Operating System

Any enterprise develops a management operating system. This is the system of linkages between different components of the operation by which the different departments and operating units communicate with each other, and by which management directs the operation and receives information on its performance. Usually there is little formal design of the management operating system — it springs up spontaneously as units begin to operate and management to manage, and incorporates each new directive and procedure as the enterprise evolves.

This casual and agglomerative system assembly procedure serves well, because it captures decisions and occurrences and builds a library of experience such that similar issues can be handled in the same way in the future without requiring management attention. There is a degree to which routine operating matters can be guided and decided without thought, and to this degree the automatic response of the management operating system to problems is invaluable. But it is not sufficient unto itself; like the auto-pilot in an airliner, the management operating system serves to free human intelligence for the larger and less routine problems. Management intelligence is needed both to handle the non-routine occurrences, and to audit, evaluate and modify the function of the management operating system.

The management operating system should be a dynamic, directed entity orienting the day-by-day operations to today's if not tomorrow's problems. Yet by the nature of the system, it captures and stores yesterday's intelligence for reuse tomorrow. The bridge, to keep the system alive and current, is management redirection, from yesterday to today and tomorrow, and this requires a management that comprehends both the changes that tomorrow's operations will require, and the practical art of accomplishing those changes smoothly so that today's operations are not disrupted. This management component requires a strategic overview in order to function effectively, and is itself a key element of strategic overview management.

Structure, And Work Planning

Routine operations deal with the combination of current requirements and accustomed habit patterns. The habit patterns are a part of the building of a sound, productive routine. Also, these habit patterns become central to the operation and must be respected.

One key element in work planning for any group is the issue of what should be fixed, and what variable. Most managements work out a pattern of things that are usually the same — these are the elements of the routine procedures — and design this pattern to accommodate variable elements as they most frequently occur. The human personality has keyed into it a certain requirement for structure, and a certain resistance to change. Both traits were survival requirements for the primitive tribes from which human civilization later developed. In a modern organization the same traits are still important factors governing behavior.

An automobile assembly plant developed a smooth, repetitive procedure for the painting of automobile wheels — the operator purged his spray gun, reconnected a paint hose, sprayed four wheels, and repeated the procedure. But the procedure design, with a built-in clean-out and reconnection after each four wheels, meant that the operator could change color for each car by connecting a different hose, without varying the preset routine. Because color was designed into this procedure as a variable, a possibility for a change in color with every car had been built in, without any change in procedure.

In the same way that an automotive engineer planned the wheel-painting routine in this way, almost every job has elements where change is automatic and accepted, and others which seem always to stay the same. A shipping room has a fixed order picking, packing and handling routine — but bases it on the assumption that no two orders may be the same, and each can be shipped to a different address.

Keeping The Structure Flexible

Thus operating management has always a set of routine procedures with built-in variables. Changes in these variables are assumed as a part of the operation. Changes in the procedures themselves must be made with care and planning, because the procedures become a part of the familiar structure which the group clings to and protects — as a remote remnant of the way in which our primitive forefathers clung to and protected the procedures for living on which the survival of the tribe depended.

Operating management also has its familiar procedures to which it clings. And, within the normal concentration barriers of operating management, reasons for changes in management's own familiar procedures almost never assert themselves. This is why a strategic overview is so essential here.

From a strategic overview, management can establish and imbue the concept that all procedures are open to change — that reevaluation is constant and ongoing — perhaps that organization members can participate in planning changes and redesign affecting them directly — that the threat of change will be moderated by wise management action — but that the organizational norm will be one of active preparation for moving into the future.

To make a plan for management of corporate operations, and to accomplish the dynamic management pattern suggested above, the services of the foresight function discussed earlier are again invaluable. Someone must track events in the outside world, making the bridge to establish relevance when it exists, and calling the event or trend to the attention of the operating managers concerned with this component of strategic overview planning. Operating management could do its own environmental search — but usually does not, for lack of time in the face of the normal operating pressures. The key is to gather the information for operating management to use to make a plan and act on it.

The Dynamics Of The Management Operating System

Each of the major functions of management — planning, organizing, staffing, directing and controlling — has its component elements and procedures, as does the management operating system itself. Each of these procedures should be considered for its potential vulnerability to impact of outside events.

90

The comparison is with parallel procedures and processes, and the potential application of new technology from any potential source. The vulnerability is to events in the flow of social, political and technological change in which the organization and its external environment are immersed.

The plan that is needed, for the management of corporate operations, should attempt to absorb and adapt to these external change processes. By so doing, it continually manages and redirects the inertia of the organization as it rolls forward into the future, and shifts direction and emphasis in that way most appropriate to keep the corporate operations current, effective, productive and competitive in an ever-more-demanding world.

CHAPTER XI

THE MANAGEMENT OF SELF-RENEWAL

A major organizational task is the management of the self-renewal of that organization. In order that this task can be accomplished management must comprehend the scope and import of the self-renewal need, and plan for its accomplishment. As with other major management tasks, the primary planning task responsibility lies with the line managers who have the power to lay action out in advance and take responsibility for its accomplishment. And as with other major planning tasks, the effectiveness of the line management effort can be greatly enhanced by effective staff support.

The Self-Renewal Tasks

Organizational self-renewal is the process by which an organization maintains its vitality and effectiveness beyond the tenure of its human components, to a theoretical potential for an infinite life span. Just as biochemists point to a continual exchange of specific chemical entities so that a given molecule of the body will be rebuilt with new materials, so the specific human elements of an organization change with hiring, firing, promotions, retirements, resignations, and all of the other reasons why one person may replace another in a job. But in spite of this chemical interchange process most higher life forms go through a life cycle. They mature, age and die. The biological exchange processes are not sufficient in span to keep all elements of every molecule renewed. The total biological structure ages.

The organizational self-renewal task is that of defining the ways in which an organization can age, in that elements become less relevant and less effective, and in finding ways in which this aging process can be overcome by specific management action.

An organization ages in part by formalization, as the connective procedures become over-rigid. It ages also in problem-solving. As problems recur and become familiar they can be fitted into categories, with a solution for each. As the categories become familiar, problem-solving becomes more and more routine and less cerebral. This is satisfactory so long as the nature of the problems does not change. But over time the nature of problems always changes, and one risk of aging is the risk of continuing to use a preplanned set of problem solutions after they cease perfectly to fit the problems.

Synergistic Processes: Management Of Opportunity And Self-Renewal

There is an overlap between the plan for the management of organizational self-renewal and the plan for management of corporate operations and the overlap is a reinforcement to both. Where the concern of the operations plan is with keeping all areas of corporate operations and the systems which link them current and forward-oriented, self-renewal deals with the organic structure of the management operating system and of the organization itself, and the qualifications of the people who staff it at all levels — and attempts to guide the evolution and recreation of this system, so that it stays continually vital, strong and effective in spite of the aging of people and the changing of requirements.

At lower levels in the organization the effective functioning of the plan for the management of the corporate organization eliminates the need for a separate self-renewal effort, because both ask many of the same questions, and the need of both to look into the future is about the same. But at the upper levels, the self-renewal efforts must deal with longer time horizons, and the difference between the two plans becomes quite large.

The Top Level Self-Renewal Need

The need and the risks in case of strategic blindness or other failure are highest at the upper corporate levels of the line and in key staff or other assignments. The people in these positions both directly determine the corporate future as the business evolves, and indirectly determine that future through hiring decisions and through design of corporate systems and procedures. With the same decision makers governing both processes, failures in their perceptions are likely to result in compounded errors. If a missed variable unexpectedly disrupts current programs, in so doing it is likely to make demands for managerial knowledge and experience the corporation has also failed to acquire.

For example, the onset of heavy financial penalties for Equal Employment Opportunity compliance failures caught some companies by surprise, even though the requirement was not new and compliance pressure had been building. These companies were forced into immediate creation of a significant, acceptable program in an area where none of the management group knew what the requirements were, how an effective EEO program should be designed, or how to manage it without disrupting relationships with the existing employee group. Strategic blindness, in not perceiving that this was a new law which had to be obeyed, caused these companies both to pay severe penalties for past behavior and to disrupt ongoing operations in a disorderly attempt at instant compliance. They had both put off consideration of this problem and failed to gather the competence to deal with it when it became a crisis.

An Open System

An organization and its management operating system together form a complex open system, with all of the normal open system characteristics.[1] One of these characteristics is the requirement for energy input from outside of the system boundaries, to prevent function and performance from degrading.

In the specific case of an organization and its management operating system, this energy input requirement is the management intervention and guidance necessary to keep the system functioning at peak efficiency against changing requirements. A well-run enterprise rarely has major reorganizations, because it does not need them. It does not need them because the need for organizational changes never accumulates. Management is continually making small adjustments in response to need — so that relatively major shifts in structure, or increases or decreases in personnel, are accomplished quietly and almost unnoticed.

But this requires a steady input of management energy from outside of the open system — that is, from outside of the routine components of the operation. If a management seeks for a strategic overview, as advocated here, it attains a position outside of the operating routine from which such adjustments can be made, and its plan for organizational self-renewal can fulfill the open system requirement for an energy input which will keep the organization and the system functioning efficiently, effectively and productively for the indefinite future.

Solving Problems At The Top

The greatest difficulty a management has in dealing with needed change in the organization and in the management operating system is in the area where top management itself is both the judge of the need for change and the factor in the system being evaluated. It is hard for the members of a top management group to be objective either about the efficiency and effectiveness of their own individual functioning, or about shifts in the future requirements which could make their skills less relevant and could call for experience and knowledge which they do not possess.

In many cases the only way in which a management serious about the long-term viability of the enterprise can accomplish a sufficiently detached strategic overview to permit a self-renewal plan to be adequate to the need is by delegating this analysis to an outside committee. Sometimes members of the board of directors have a sufficient knowledge and a sufficient detachment from the operating routine so that they can carry out this portion of the planning. In other cases it is necessary to turn to outside professionals.

In any case this is a task whose delegation must be handled with care, in spite of the urgency of getting the job done and done well. No management will be comfortable in creating a review committee to make organizational self-renewal recommendations involving their own future, and will wish to keep some control over the committee. Yet the professionals with this assignment will not feel comfortable in making forthright recommendations which could be adverse to some of the managers who will judge the report and authorize payment for it. The most viable compromise can be supervision of such organizational self-renewal evaluation by a committee of the board of directors, preferably a committee both strong enough to guide the task well and sufficiently removed from routine operations to judge from a reasonably neutral position.

Society's Need For Corporate Self-Renewal

The corporation as a legal form through which business is accomplished is essentially eternal. It need never cease to function if its parts are kept up to date and well-integrated with each other and with the customers, suppliers and others on which the business depends.

Not only is the corporation theoretically capable of eternal life, but it assumes a role in society which should require it to function indefinitely. The social responsibility elements which were bypassed earlier through management of corporate social impact mostly require a business with an eternal life.

The community depends on the business — not only this year and next year, but forever. The employees depend on the business for continued employment; while they will age and retire, by then others will take their place, and the dependency will go on — either forever, or until the business defaults on its maintenance of the expected ties. And the same is true of customer expectations for continued supply of their favorite products, or supplier expectations that the firm will continue to buy the custom products which were tailored to fit its needs, and so forth. Society needs and hopes for business firms which last forever.

The stockholders and managers have an even larger stake in a continuing business. And the means to long business life is through careful planning, by constructing a plan for organizational self-renewal and then putting this plan into action — not as a one-time exercise, but as a steady, gentle paring and reshaping, to keep the organization and the management operating system always current, lean and effective.

FOOTNOTES

[1]Daniel Katz and Robert L. Kahn, *The Social Psychology of Organizations,* John Wiley & Sons, New York 1966, Chapter 2.

CHAPTER XII

INFORMATION REQUIREMENTS FROM THE CORPORATE ENVIRONMENT

Strategic overview management as outlined in the preceding chapters requires the preparation of five interrelated plans — for the management of social impact, opportunity, course correction, operations and self-renewal, all from a strategic overview perspective. All five also require a special gathering of information, so that decisions which can be kept timely due to the overview perspective are informed decisions, and of the highest possible quality.

As stated earlier, line management lives in the present, doing the best possible job on today's decisions, given the information available — and it becomes a staff job to look ahead to tomorrow's decision needs, to attempt to anticipate the information which necessary decisions will require, to gather or otherwise acquire this information, to analyze and organize it, and to have it ready for line management to assimilate and consider as each decision process begins to mature and decision-time approaches. This chapter will consider that information process, and relate it to the other elements of the planning system, the management operating system and the strategic overview management process.

The Corporate Environment As A Study In Patterns

One of the most dramatic among the many changes in the demands on business management in recent decades has been the rapid growth in the importance of forces and events in the world outside of the corporation. These forces and events may come as reactions to specific corporate actions, may challenge long established operating practices, or may bring acceptance of profitable new products or services.

The first and broadest level for corporate concern about the environment is at the level of social structures and patterns. Thomas Kuhn pointed out the tendency for new theories and views to be sharply repressed by the established views, until a final moment of acceptance when there is an abrupt shift; the new becomes the established theory. The old theory is ridiculed, and there is a casual restatement of history to show that the acceptance of the new was a gradual process; everyone conveniently forgets that it was ever rejected. After a lapse of time it becomes difficult to reconstruct the abruptness of the shift from acceptance of the old to acceptance of the new and rejection of the old. Thus major changes in scientific thinking have occurred with surprising suddenness now forgotten. This sudden shift from one pattern of perception to another Kuhn refers to as a paradigm shift.[1]

Social changes move in the same way, and in retrospect it is often forgotten that the actual change from one pattern to another was abrupt and traumatic. Today's world is preparing for a long series of pattern shifts, or paradigm shifts, as illustrated by the elements in the *Limits To Growth* controversy.

The book, *Limits To Growth*[2], reported the results of a computer modeling project, sponsored by the Club of Rome, carried out at MIT using Jay Forrester's systems dynamics approach to project the future of the world — a future of limited growth; hence the title. Projections of the continued expansion of population and industry showed the world as reaching the limits both of food supply and of basic environmental systems. Over a rather wide range of growth rates the outcome was almost identical — a projection that after another fifty to eighty years there would be a collapse, with world population falling to half or two-thirds of the present level.

The book stirred a large controversy. However, most of the serious critics accepted the broad thrust of the study, saying either that the limits to growth and subsequent collapse would not be so imminent if the equations had been defined in some different way, or that mankind is too intelligent to allow unlimited growth to proceed to the point of such a system collapse. Behind the controversy, and supported in viewpoints of the study and of most of its critics, is the perception that a major change in world lifestyles is impending and will occur, at least in the major industrial countries. The details of this change are unclear, but it is likely to involve the way that world resources are used, the rate at which heat energy is released by combustion and nuclear reactions, and the production and consumption of food. This change will, in ways yet unspecified, represent a paradigm shift, a fundamental change in patterns of industry and commerce based on changes in the ways that people live and work.

Signs of a paradigm shift within the individual sectors of the economy are manifest. The legal evolution which led to the Clean Waters Act has set in motion a substantial change in the industrial and municipal use of water. The OPEC influence on the price of oil has changed economic patterns of several countries and brought sooner the pangs of eventual exhaustion of a limited resource. Changes in regulations have shifted the operation patterns of several industries. The intense competitive pressure on the steel industry from newer and more technologically advanced industries in Japan and Europe has started a restructuring, to the point that the U.S. industry is likely to be entirely different in its nature within a generation.

These industry paradigms are undoubtedly elements in some larger pattern not yet clear. The importance is not the precise nature of this larger pattern, but the immediate impact on individual businesses. The major threat to any corporation from the outside environment is the risk of being caught and crushed by a major shift of the social and competitive framework within which that business operates. Another and almost equally potent incentive for careful and continuing study of developing paradigms is the creation of new business opportunities by the same shifts.

The first need, therefore, is for study of the social, political, and economic systems relevant to any business, to establish the types of shifts which are impending and the likelihood that either problems or opportunities will merge as a result within a relevant span of time. The time component of this analysis is important, both because the stresses that cause such shifts build slowly over long periods of time, and because the actual changes in pattern are sometimes quite abrupt and traumatic.

The slow growth in stresses in the earth's crust leads ultimately to an earthquake. Scientists can measure the increase in stresses and estimate the increasing probability of an earthquake, but cannot as yet predict the specific time or severity. In the same way, stress built slowly in the steel markets, to the present crisis level.

During the intervals between crises this whole issue of shifts in patterns can safely be ignored, just as the people of Pompeii could ignore Mount Vesuvius for generation after generation. This is a matter of business risk — the expense of careful study of the paradigm-shift potential and relevance is a steady investment of the current funds of the business, repaid only in case of an eruption successfully forecast. Unlike a volcanic eruption, most of the paradigm shifts of the business world are benign enough so that the astute can make advantage out of an event which otherwise might jeopardize the existence of the business. This is the justification for concern with the paradigm shift issue for a survival-oriented business, versus a much more casual attitude from businesses that feel that the risks are more remote.

Routine Operating Information

The routine components of the planning process need a steady flow of routine operating information — either the raw operating

99

data, or reports presenting, summarizing and analyzing this data for planning and management. The information requirement is a normal part of any management control system, as well as of the planning system and the management operating system of which it is a part.

The only question about routine information is the organizational protocol issue of who gathers the information, who analyzes, and who shares the reports and analyses which result. The planning function has no need to specialize in information gathering and report preparation, unless no one else will do it — and other members of the organization, such as the controller's staff or the data processing department, may have a jealous grip on the right to handle the numbers and send reports to management. This is only a problem if the analysis and reporting is not timely or competent, or if information is withheld from those who need it for their planning. Then Planning is forced to become involved either in obtaining a rationalizing of the reporting process, or if this is not feasible, in gathering and reporting information necessary for planning otherwise not available to line managers.

Planning Information

Routine planning information differs from routine operating information in that it deals not with the current operations, but with the routine reporting of the other variables normally considered in the course of plan formulation. For example, almost every organization has a system by which information on the markets into which it sells is gathered and reported — most commonly by a market research group attached to the sales or marketing function of the business selling into that market. Another sort of information is the routine forecast of economic variables, often issued by the corporate economist if there is one, which is intended to provide a common basis for the planning of the different elements of a diverse firm.

If the information needs can be satisfied by reports from an existing department, such as the market research unit, then this is the best and most efficient process. However, if no organizational unit exists to supply certain information, the planning function often finds itself either as the purchaser of an outside service or the gatherer and reporter of specialized information.

This is a default option, but common. For example, a corporation that does not have its own economics department may receive forecast information from its planning unit, because it is necessary to have standardized economic assumptions in the plans. Thus, a planning function often will be the genesis of new types of routine reports — which may eventually result in the spin-off of new staff departments, such as an economics unit.

The summary thought here is that the planning unit has the task of facilitating effective and efficient planning by its line management, and should be careful that it does not drift too far from this task. Some routine reporting is a desirable transition, to get new information in front of the management, but usually Planning is stronger and more effective in the long run if it does not take on too many corollary operating tasks, such as issuing routine reports.

Non-Routine Planning Information

A normal and proper part of the work of any planning function is to find, develop and report new types of information which line management may find useful in the course of its planning. Planning continually is searching, gathering and reporting. A part of the task of the function is to explore proposed new information sources, and most planning directors will cultivate a flow of information about new services from information vendors of all sorts.

A potential jurisdictional conflict exists, in that marketing research or other staff units also should explore new information sources, and often have active programs to do so. The conflict never arises if Planning is able to draw on such a group as an information source, rather than competing with it internally. A strong partnership often develops, where Planning may budget discretionary funds to aid such a unit in financing the trial of new services.

This sort of a sharing works well, if Planning carries only a portion of the cost. As with most other things, if the other unit gets the service 'free' — that is, if Planning pays the entire cost — it may not feel any real commitment to make the trial succeed, or may let the priority of other projects interfere with the evaluation. Planning has a large stake in the results and sometimes a strong role in getting new information flows started, but often serves its own and the corporation's interests best if it starts new things, shifts to a partnership with one of the staff units, and then withdraws as the information begins to find routine use.

The new-information finding role of the planning function requires an information search process. Some organization of this information search by definition of a new-events scanning horizon usually makes it more productive, and thus increases the planning functions contribution and value.

THE NEW-EVENTS SCANNING HORIZON. The concept of a new-events scanning horizon is that of a boundary in time and relevance. Every search process requires boundaries of some sort, in order to define the effort and permit it to be organized effectively. In this case the boundaries are of three types: (I) areas of automatic significance, (II) limits to normal relevance, and (III) outreaches, to watch for new trends or new types of events, and to confirm that the limits to normal relevance are still set correctly.

By areas of automatic significance are meant those zones around the business where past important external events have had their origin. For example, in the history of strip mining the Indiana Coal Association provides one of the better chapters. Before World War II the Indiana industry leaders saw the need for a major reclamation effort, a growing public agitation for action, and competitive barriers to initiatives by any one company. The solution was political, with industry sponsorship of a series of legislative acts requiring land reclamation to an extent which was increased several times over the years.

But having opened the door to this sort of regulation, the Association was vulnerable to increased requirements, and many environmental groups wished stricter rules or a total prohibition of surface mining. The Association kept careful track of events in this area — and its new-events scanning horizon assigned automatic relevance to any proposed legislation affecting mining or reclamation in any way, and to related actions or statements by members of the legislature or state administration.

Many corporations and industries have legislative or regulatory areas of interest of this same sort, and follow events there with great care, because of past experience with developments of great importance and relevance.

The Indiana Coal Association had, in partnership with the legislature, guided the evolution of the strip-mining of coal to a better balance with the environment than elsewhere in the U.S., but even though flagrant abuses in other states continued to stir public indignation, proposals for federal regulation drew little support.

By themselves, restrictions on strip-mining have never become enough of a national issue to bring enactment of new federal laws. But as time passed and the public became thoroughly aroused over stream pollution and other sorts of environmental degradation, federal legislation began to emerge — first dealing directly with water and air pollution, but eventually extending to many other areas including surface mining, and putting specific and stringent requirements nationwide on the strip-mining of coal. A company following this process would have started by classifying the agitation for federal legislation at the extreme fringe but within the limits to potential relevance and therefore worth monitoring. Then year by year this area would have been classified as potentially more important as the pressure built, until the federal law passed and superseded the earlier state regulations.

From the standpoint of the same coal company, the events in the oil world were too remote for relevance for many years. After World War II low-cost oil had taken away the railroad and home-heating markets from the coal industry, and a significant portion of the central power station market, and the shift seemed permanent. But the (III) outreach element of new-events scanning would have kept a general touch with the oil industry outlook. The specific year of the oil crisis may not have been predictable, but the long term growth in the demand for coal could have been anticipated through outreach studies.

For the better planning functions the definition of these new events scanning horizons are clear and sharp, since a focusing of effort is necessary for effectiveness. In seeking to improve a planning function or in establishing a new one, the time required to define these scanning horizons is well repaid by the results.

Within the first of the suggested horizons were the areas of automatic significance — the regulatory and political areas, the market areas, the social and community contacts, where past experience and present knowledge confirm that new events and trends are likely to have relevance and a significant impact — these are the areas where a large portion of the available scanning resources will be concentrated.

These are also areas whose importance often justifies the creation of specialized staffs — for marketing research, for the legislative interface, for community relations, for regulatory affairs, for EEO compliance, and so forth. Planning could find itself in an unproductive competition over the monitoring of some of these areas — where a cooperative effort best serves the corporate interest, with the specialized staff doing its own job and sharing the resulting information — and Planning supplementing this through its own efforts and in turn sharing the results.

In new-events scanning beyond the areas of automatic relevance Planning will normally be the primary monitor, since the other staffs will be constrained by near-term issues and budgetary pressures from working this far out. Still the partnership cited in the previous paragraph is needed, so that there is no misunderstanding of the Planning role, and the other groups are secure in the knowledge that they will receive any information of possible relevance to them.

SELECTING PLANNING INFORMATION SERVICES.
Basically Planning needs to map out the areas which seem poten-

tially relevant and locate information flows such that new developments can be tracked without excessive effort. The most appropriate information sources will vary according to the nature and focus of the business.

However, the list will probably include standard suppliers such as SRI International[3] and Arthur D. Little[4] whose planning information services are widely used by major corporations. Both services provide a flow of survey reports profiling new developments in specific industry areas, as well as changes in the economic or social framework in which business is being conducted. Both aim to provide a good briefing document for introduction to a new area, and then offer specialized consulting services as a supplement.

Beyond this sort of survey service, businesses with interests in the consumer market place or in social and lifestyle variables will want to consider services such as the Yankelovich Monitor[5] which profiles these trends, or Opinion Research,[6] an ADL subsidiary, which offers a parallel service less detailed but more oriented to management briefing.

Many staffs will also want econometric information and projections, and will wish to consider Data Resources,[7] Chase Econometrics,[8] Wharton[9] or another service. What these and other similar services provide is a combination of written economic forecasts, and access to a major econometric model. Many clients purchase on-line computer access to the model, and use the simulation capabilities to correlate their own business variables to factors in the model. Some build smaller derivative models to translate the major forecasts into estimates of how their own business areas will be impacted.

These are very useful techniques, with the limitation that econometric modeling is a science only with regard to past occurrences, and an art where the future is involved — so that all future projections must be qualified by the inherent limitations of economic models which still require small design changes with every new turn of the economy. Such models are of great value — so long as they are taken as probable estimates of trends, rather than specific and factual predictions.

The preceding services are a few of the basic ones which most planning functions will wish to evaluate. Beyond them are an almost infinite array of more specialized or individualized services, for many consultants and market research organizations compete aggressively for Planning interest. A significant call on the time of the planning director or a delegate is in evaluating the more promising proposals, since both budgetary limitations and the limits on the ability to absorb the information set a ceiling on the number of subscriptions which can be entered among the almost infinite variety of offerings.

Two specialized service areas deserve mention. One is the general inquiry area — where a service such as Find[10] offers to answer unspecified questions for general or specific information quickly and as they arise, or computer access to major information databases such as ABI-Inform[11] or Lockheed[12] allow rapid literature search and abstract retrieval in specific areas, and Washington Researchers[13] offers expert access to federal government publications and data.

The other specialized area is the study of the future itself, where organizations such as the Futures Group[14] or the Center for Futures Research[15] help corporations to anticipate future trends and events in specific areas — the former in addition to certain general services focuses on helping a client to analyze and understand future trends in that company's own business areas, and the latter works through a series of major annual studies, each sponsored by a group of participating corporate clients.

The end result of several years of evaluation of different services, plus a trial of some of the more promising candidates, should be the development of a few basic sources which the planning group learns to use well, plus a continual overlayment of specialized studies, multi-client searches and individual investigations of areas of present interest. At a given time the non-routine projects would cover both specific new-event scanning areas which seemed to warrant the extra attention, and probes into the areas beyond the normal limits of relevance, to keep alert for new developments and to adjust the scanning boundaries as necessary.

The choice of services is individual to a company or group both because needs differ from firm to firm, and because the different services require different investments in client time and skill in order to use them effectively. The cost of any service is the total of the internal and external charges for using it, and this must be matched against the benefit to a specific firm with a specific array of other information resources and suppliers.

THE FORESIGHT ROLE. In Chapter V the concept of a foresight function was discussed. This is a grouping of all of the components of the planning information search as a separate function, which works with and for all of the corporate components with futures information needs. The foresight activity can be organized as a component of the planning function, or as a related group. If the foresight function is a part of Planning, the preceding discussion applies directly. If the foresight function is separate, then it instead of Planning must assume the leadership in information search and in developing an effective partnership with the other staffs. In this case Planning would be concerned only with special studies in areas of its current interest, and would need to help guide and define the general information overview objectives.

ENVIRONMENTAL SCANNING SYSTEMS. There are three basic approaches to the necessary overview of the corporate environment. One is simply to purchase outside services, and to attempt to integrate this information with the internal planning process. As discussed earlier, the limitations of this approach have led many corporations to establish a foresight function or its equivalent. The foresight staff can then operate by setting up its own surveillance of the external environment, or by catalyzing the formation of an environmental scanning system through which the organization itself becomes involved in and aware of relevant external trends.

The various scanning systems largely are derived directly or indirectly from work done at the Institute of Life Insurance, leading to the TAP program, a trend analysis system developed by a group headed by Arnold Brown and Edith Weiner, which was used successfully by the Institute membership in developing new industry programs in response to outside pressures. The success of this work was well publicized, and subsequently a new firm was founded by former members of the ILI staff to aid corporations and other organizations in establishing a parallel form of environmental scanning system within the client organization.[16]

The concept of such a system is that various members of the organization — preferably from a wide variety of departments and organizational levels — volunteer to scan specific publications for specific types of events. One volunteer might be assigned to read *Scientific American* for new social developments potentially relevant to the future of that organization, and another volunteer might also be assigned to read *Scientific American*, but for relevant new technology.

As discussed in Chapter V, certain publications tend to be leaders, in that they carry new ideas and developments sooner than others. A list of these publications is developed, starting from the experience at ILI and elsewhere, and then tailored to the needs and interests of the specific client. From this roster of publications and the variety of different viewpoints from which they are to be screened, a potential information matrix is created, and the volunteers recruited to gather the information to fill it. Volunteers receive free subscriptions and management attention as a result of their activity. But a major incentive is involvement in a new dimension, as most of the scanning assignments are intentionally design-

106

ed to lead the volunteer to read outside of his or her normal reading pattern and from a different viewpoint.

The result of all of this reading is a stream of abstracts — each volunteer is asked to write a brief summary of each relevant item, stating what it is and why it is potentially important. These abstracts go to an analysis committee, of individuals with strong analytical ability chosen from the groups most interested in the scanning system output. The job of the analysis committee is to screen the abstracts for signs of relevant developing patterns.

Any important new development or trend is likely to be reported from several sources and with increasing frequency as its importance grows. Where the scanning signals such a trend, and the analysis committee feels that this is a potentially significant development, it reports this result to a policy committee. This is a committee of managers chosen to be representative of the groups participating in the scanning system, and the policy committee then recommends management action where this seems appropriate.

All of this is a lot of discussion and procedure, and it consumes a significant amount of the time of members of the organization. Its justification is a proven ability to get the entire technical and managerial staff of an organization involved in and aware of outside developments. With this level of awareness and interest, most external challenges will be anticipated long before the event, and the potential for creative solutions to problems originating outside of the organization is at a maximum. Where a high level of organizational involvement is desired, this approach to fulfilling a significant portion of the organization's external information needs is an excellent one.[17,18]

Information For Planning

The objective of all of this information search effort is a cost-effective information flow, to the other staffs who need the information service in order to perform their proper roles, and to the line management. The information to management is, of course, the more crucial role, and requires both planning and judgment from the staff, since the preparation for a given decision often must start six months or a year in advance, if adequate information is to be gathered, and yet the staff cannot know with certainty when unexpected events may precipitate a decision, and cannot expend the budget necessary to be always prepared for any possible decision. Usually, however, a reasonable efficiency is possible, in preparing for necessary decisions in a timely way without too often spending time and resources on reports and efforts which are never needed.

The information needs of the organization, the management operating system, and the top management group specifically are of critical importance to effective function and quality decisions. The challenge to the planning group and to the planning director or to the head of the foresight function is to meet this challenge in a cost/effective way, and to meet it well enough to make a competitive advantage out of the quality of information on which the decisions are based.

FOOTNOTES

[1]Thomas Kuhn, *Theory Of Scientific Revolution,* 2nd Edition, enlarged, University of Chicago Press, 1970.

[2]Donella H. Meadows, Dennis L. Meadows, Jorgen Randers and William Behrens, *Limits To Growth,* Universe Books, New York, 1972.

[3]Business Intelligence Program, SRI International, 333 Ravenswood Avenue, Menlo Park, California 94025.

[4]ADL Impact Service, Arthur D. Little, Inc., Acorn Park, Cambridge, Massachusetts 02140.

[5]Yankelovich, Skelly & White, 575 Madison Avenue, New York, New York 10022.

[6]Opinion Research Corporation, North Harrison, Princeton, New Jersey 08540.

[7]Data Resources, Inc., 29 Hartwell Avenue, Lexington, Massachusetts 02171.

[8]Chase Econometrics, 555 City Line Avenue, Bala Cynwyd, Pennsylvania 19004.

[9]Wharton Econometric Forecasting Associates, Inc., 369 Lexington Avenue, New York, New York 10017.

[10]Find/SVP, 500 Fifth Avenue, New York, New York 10036.

[11]ABI-Inform Database, Data Courier, Inc., 620 S. Fifth Street, Louisville, Kentucky 40202.

[12]Lockheed Information Systems, 200 Park Avenue, New York, New York 10017.

[13]Washington Researchers, 910 Seventeenth Street NW, Washington DC 20006.

[14]The Futures Group, 76 Eastern Boulevard, Glastonbury, Connecticut 06033.

[15]Center For Futures Research, Graduate School of Business Administration, University of Southern California, Los Angeles, California 90007.

[16]Weiner, Edrich & Brown, 303 Lexington Avenue, Lobby C, New York, New York 10016.

[17]Arnold Brown, "Society's Ravelled Sleeve: A Perspective on The Planner's Dilemma," *Planning Review,* September 1979, pp. 13-17.

[18]"Firm Helping Bosses Focus on the Future," *The Wall Street Journal,* October 5, 1981, pp 31⁺.

CHAPTER XIII

TECHNOLOGY AND TECHNICAL PLANNING

Technology is the underlying fabric of modern society. But, while the warp and woof of other fabrics stays constant once laid down, technology shifts continually. Fortunately, technology shifts in a way that is at least partly predictable.

Once there were high technology businesses and low technology businesses. Now all major businesses are high technology businesses, due to the way in which technical devices and systems have penetrated our society. Businesses do differ in whether they create new technology, as in the semiconductor field, or apply the technology created by others, as in modern retailing. Effective management requires an understanding of the degree to which a specific business is vulnerable to shifts in technology and whether shifts are likely, and a business dependent on the creation of new technology needs to give specific attention to the management of the process.

A management familiar with the impacts of technology can readily understand the possibility and importance of technology changes, but this does not necessarily mean that those managers will perceive the threats to their own positions. Through a narrowness in point of view, management sometimes accepts the possibility of all other changes except the risk that a better technology might replace that business' own key discovery. Technical planning is fraught with such perception problems, some caused by the bias of ignorance where change comes unexpectedly, and some caused by the bias of a narrow horizon.

At some point in time automated checkout systems and instant electronic payment for purchases seem likely to be broadly applied by retail stores. Both are technical developments of high ultimate probability but slow to arrive. Together they will have profound impacts on retailing, which has traditionally been a low technology area. But the vulnerability of this or any other business to a shift in technology is not related to the level of technology presently employed, only to the impact of those applications potential in its future. As automated checkout, inventory, payment, and merchandise security systems, or cable TV sales systems, aid some retailers in operating more efficiently or effectively, the retail businesses as a group will abruptly increase their level of applied technology, and will change significantly as a consequence. As this change finally occurs, some retailers, ignorant of the potential for technology change or not convinced of its imminence, will be caught unprepared.

Social Change As The Driving Force

The protection of the business against upsets due to new technology requires timely management decisions based in part on technical, social and market information. Such information can be gathered by a foresight activity as discussed in Chapter IX, as it examines new developments and the trends that they represent in order to anticipate impact and opportunity. Such a function was once more narrowly conceived as technological forecasting, but while that discipline and its tools still fully apply, a broader horizon is now required.

The fundamental determinants of new business opportunity are (I) new technology, (II) changes in demographics, currencies and world economics, and (III) social change.[1] An effective foresight function must consider all three. While technology is the critical variable for development of new products, social factors often determine whether anyone will buy them. Social change is frequently the driving force behind major shifts in market demand, and its impact often stimulates the investment, as technology is applied to generate new products and services. No longer is the existence of new technology sufficient to create a market. The technology for electronic funds transfer has been perfected for some time but social variables related to consumer acceptability, privacy and potential for theft appear to control the progress, and actual adoption is coming only gradually.

In the same way that social changes shift demand and surface new needs, demographic shifts from region to region or from age group to age group cause markets to dry up and others to flourish. Changes in currencies signal shifts in comparative advantage which benefit some countries more than others. Secular changes in world economics, as crude oil and foodstuffs rise in price for example, cause shifts in other needs and in trade patterns.

Technology represents a means to a specific end, in terms of a potentially useful process, product or service. But the fact of the potential is not enough. Technical planning requires verification that a driving force also exists which will cause that potential to be applied. Such a driving force comes from the market place. The market place is subject to major shifts with social change, and demographic, currency and world economic change. Thus, the foresight function which judges process, product or service development potential must also comprehend these variables in order to be effective.

Applied Technology And R&D Management

THE ROLE OF TECHNOLOGY. Technology once was a primary driving force for change. In the earlier period of the industrial revolution the fact that someone had discovered a device representing a technical solution to a problem was sufficient justification to build and market it. Today, while the technical solution is still a necessary part of the equation, society may restrict its introduction, or simply refrain from buying the resulting product or service if it does not fit with ongoing trends.

Population growth has also been a past major driving force, in bringing new and ever-larger markets. Today population growth is much slower, except for demographic shifts, many of which are derivatives of social change. Thus social change, which has always been a driving variable, emerges as the most important of the three — acting independently to create new opportunities, or acting to govern population shifts or to encourage and approve a shift to new technology. This dominance of the social change variable has reached the point where an indication of potential social and market acceptability of a potential new technical development is usually a wise preliminary to the funding of the actual research and development work which will produce the technical solution.

TECHNICAL PLANNING. The purpose of technical planning is to anticipate and to satisfy the technical needs of the organization with an array of technical products, processes, devices and services which are designed, developed, or otherwise obtained in order to have them available and operative as needed. For internal needs, as in electronic checkout or inventory control, this is a foresight, design, development, installation, operation program. For external needs, as in creating a new generation of microcomputers, this is a foresight, discovery, design, development, production, marketing program. The operation of technical planning is as a component of corporate or strategic planning — developed first perhaps as a derivative plan and then integrated — dealing with the means of anticipating, finding or developing the necessary technology, and attaining by internal or external effort the necessary conversion into technical processes, products, devices or services, as required for fulfillment of the strategic plan.

The foresight component of technical planning deals with the understanding of the possible match between the technical potentials which exist and the needs of and threats to the organization.

This requires a circular process starting with a tentative definition of technology development potentials relevant to the organization, followed by a survey of these and related technology frontiers, redefinition of technology development potentials, and resurvey of the knowledge frontiers — with a continual iteration and a continuous alertness for new relevance of any new knowledge.

A number of years often elapse between the discovery which established the technical potential for a given development, and the actual creation of the device — as, the atomic bomb became a theoretical possibility with Einstein's definition of the $E = MC^2$ equation, but became the basis for serious R&D effort only later during World War II. Therefore, for successful technical planning the group must move beyond discovering the existence of technical potentials to judgment as to the most probable rates of development and time of emergence of various new devices.

This is hard but not impossible. While definitive judgments on when a new invention will emerge are not easy, it is often possible to judge whether or not it is receiving serious R&D attention, and to gauge progress from scientific papers, testing of prototypes and so forth. A serious technical planning function makes the effort to estimate this progress wherever the result will have a significant impact on the business.

Technical planning for the internal operations which use technology developed by others require a compounding of technical judgments as to when developments will be available and how rapidly they should be applied. If a new process control computer now under development by a vendor has the potential to establish a significant competitive advantage when fully applied to reducing processing costs, (I) what will be the scope of the startup problems — how many days, months or years will elapse before it is fully operational? (II) what will be the total investment in startup effort and expense? and (III) is it more strategic to have the first installation? Or the second or third, after others have fought with the startup?

For external developments the continual issue is optimum market penetration through innovation. The challenge is to lead with important new developments. The risks are to pioneer — to introduce new developments before there is any market for them — and to be overtaken, when someone else's major advance preempts the market. The dimension of these risks and challenges depend on a company's position and strategy. Some companies never attempt leadership — but sustain a profitable secondary market position by following after the developments introduced by the market leaders. Other companies are so well established that innovation by smaller

112

competitors is beneficial and indicates when the market is ready for the next step forward by the leader, who may already have new developments ready to market at the appropriate time.

TECHNICAL PROGRAM BOUNDARIES. When technical and market forces come together to define an opportunity or to constitute a threat to present positions which must be rebutted, the two key elements are boundary definitions and methods of approach. When both have been prescribed, actual planning of potential R&D programs becomes possible.

Definition of research program boundaries can best start with the nature of the linkage between the proposed research program and the market place, as summarized in Figure 1. New processes for existing products have a simple internal justification in the potential economic gain from continuing an ongoing effort. While the total program, including the R&D effort, needs an occasional reappraisal to confirm its long-term viability, this kind of R&D work is usually the easiest to define and justify.

Figure XIII-1

RESEARCH HORIZONS

Program Boundaries:
(1) New processes for existing products.
    (defensive or aggressive boundaries)

(2) New products to protect and extend existing market positions.
    (defensive or aggressive boundaries)

(3) New products for new sales.
    (aggressive boundaries)
    (a) to replace existing products
    (b) to gain new sales

(4) Products that create new markets.
    (aggressive boundaries)
    (a) in present business areas
    (b) in new business areas

At the next level the R&D effort is asked for new products related to existing market success — to protect and extend the line, to prolong the life of a product family, or to replace a declining member of that family. Where the process improvement project depended almost entirely on technical and economic judgment of probable success, here there is a need for specific and detailed market information also. This should be readily obtainable, considering the present market position.

113

At the third level the R&D target is in new areas in existing markets — by replacing other people's products, or by market enlargement based on superior properties or economics. A higher level of market intelligence is needed.

At the fourth level the R&D effort is aimed at products or services which will create new markets[2] — in the company's present business areas, or in entirely new ones. This level requires the greatest insight and sophistication properly to judge the potential for market creation, and the potential for recovering the investment in R&D, production, distribution, and market development. Because this level is the most difficult, it is the one where failures are most frequent and successes most dramatic and rewarding.

The point of this progression is that each higher level depends more heavily on outside market and social data, plus technical information the foresight function should itself possess. Thus, the uncertainties increase at each higher level, as well as the potential rewards. A process for an existing product can only increase the return from an existing market position. However lucrative, it can only operate within the boundaries of the present market opportunity. A product which creates new markets can open major new potential, but because it represents a move into a new area the risks and uncertainties will be much, much higher, and the information requirements for sound technical planning much, much greater.

Technical Planning And Technical Action

With planning as action laid out in advance, the specific role of technical planning is to lay out technical actions which will be implemented. Specifically, this means undertaking or otherwise participating in the development of the needed new technical products, processes, devices or services. Many companies perform their own R&D. Some contract it out to others. Yet others follow or even jointly fund work in progress elsewhere — or license or acquire the successful invention, product or company. Whatever the chosen route may be, it is important clearly to understand the relationship between a given project including its timing and its cost, and the strategic plan for the business which it is intended to benefit.

FOOTNOTES

[1]George C. Sawyer, "Social Issues and Social Change," *MSU Business Topics,* Summer 1973, pp 15-20.
[2]George C. Sawyer, "Creating Markets for New Products," *Atlanta Economic Review,* November-December 1973, pp 17-20.

CHAPTER XIV

PRODUCT AND MARKET PLANNING

When the elements of strategy were presented in Chapter V, focus was introduced as the defined relationship with the customers and market place upon which a strategy is based. This is a fundamental concept. Product strategy, service strategy or business strategy should be built from a clear definition of focus level, and an equally clear understanding of the distribution and service commitments which the different focus levels require of the vendor, if a strategy is to be effective.

This chapter will further explore the focus concept as basic to product, market business and planning, and present examples of its application.[1] It will define the stages by which a product may differ from those of competitors, and the levels of involvement with the customers' needs. But the beginning is in a clearer understanding of the nature of the product or service being offered, since the degree to which the product is differentiated from those of competitors may limit focus options, and the choice among focus options itself suggests whether differentiation may be necessary in achieving the desired relationship with the customers.

Stages Of Product Differentiation

Where products vary in uniqueness from the generic grocery offerings, which position themselves as completely standard and faceless, to spectacular named gemstones which could be identified by name almost immediately by jewelers all over the world. And while the span between these two extremes is in fact a continuum, a classification into four principal stages of differentiation serves to highlight the shift in product characteristics and to guide the planning process. These four stages of differentiation are (I) unique products, (II) strong specialties, (III) weak specialties, and (IV) commodities.

UNIQUE PRODUCTS are products for which there is no substitute, and no alternative supplier. Whether there is a substitute for a product is a matter of customer opinion, of course, and different customers will have different opinions. Where one person is looking for a painting to put on a particular wall and will accept anything attractive within a specific price range, another customer may insist on an English landscape, and yet another on a work by

Picasso. With the increasing specificity of the request the range of choice is narrowed towards a more and more unique product.

When Loctite first offered its line of adhesives as a replacement for metal lock washers, comparable adhesives were not available commercially from other sources. A metal washer could still be used for most applications, but the properties of the adhesive made possible some new assemblies where a metal washer could not be used. For these uses, the Loctite product was a unique product without substitutes.

STRONG SPECIALTIES are products available from only one vendor, and whose substitutes are sufficiently inferior that the product will be purchased at a premium price. The Loctite adhesive was originally priced to cost about the same as the metal washer it replaced, but as its properties were recognized, users developed a strong preference for it, and used it even where it did not replace a metal washer, paying more in order to get a better result.

This is the normal situation with a strong specialty product. Almost every product has substitutes, but the successful specialty products give performance sufficiently better than that of those substitutes that the purchaser will willingly pay more to get the superior result. However, the marketer should still consider the price elasticity of this preference since there is a limit to the price premium which may be imposed before significant volume is lost to admittedly inferior substitutes.

At one point the State of California made a major issue over the cost of Valium, a tranquilizer with strong specialty product characteristics, and insisted that California doctors use phenothiazine tranquilizers for public assistance patients. The phenothiazines were admittedly inferior for many patients, but the price of Valium was farther above the price of phenothiazines than the State felt that it should pay. This is an example of a strong specialty product losing market because one customer felt that the price premium was too large.

WEAK SPECIALTIES are products available from only one vendor whose properties are sufficiently better so that the weak specialty will always be chosen when the price and all other things are equal. That is, a weak specialty is a superior product whose degree of superiority is too small to justify a price premium. A weak specialty can be used to gain market share very effectively, so long as the price is the same as that of the competitors.

Most businesses that have custom formulas, special blends, or other special-for-the-customer properties are attempting to create weak specialty positions. They incur extra costs in the customizing, and must recover these by increased sales, since they normally cannot pass these costs on as a price premium.

116

Sometimes these strategies fail, with these extra costs cutting margins and yielding no extra sales — either because the special properties were not that appealing, or because the competitors matched the weak specialty with equivalent weak specialties of their own.

Sometimes these strategies succeed. Hoffmann-La Roche has strengthened its sales position in bulk vitamins by a series of special blends and formulations with weak specialty product appeal — one example are the products designed for direct compression into tablets, to simplify processing for the purchaser.

COMMODITIES are products available from many vendors, and sufficiently standardized that they may be safely bought by choosing the vendor with the best price and delivery among those who can meet the product specifications. Many metals, grains, and chemicals are commodities already, and skillful purchasers often attempt to convert specialties into commodities by establishing a clear set of specifications and inducing competitive bids.

Levels Of Focus

The levels of focus are different distances — or different degrees of involvement — between the seller and the customer or his or her business. There are seven levels of vendor offerings to his or her customers: (I) available products, (II) an available product family, (III) turnkey products, (IV) turnkey solutions, (V) packaged performance, (VI) packaged service, and (VII) craftsmanship. After reviewing these levels the interrelationship between the stages of differentiation and levels of focus will be easier to illustrate.

AVAILABLE PRODUCTS. The original thrust of the industrial revolution was simply to produce goods, and many successful businesses operate on this basis still. If a business can do something well, and more economically than its competitors, the buyers will seek it out. Efficient production is necessary, but beyond that point the marketing effort can be minimal.

Andrew Carnegie made and sold steel rails. They were good steel, and Carnegie was the low-cost producer. When necessary he would undercut his competitors' prices, and the railroads always made a point of seeking him out when they needed to buy a large quantity of rails. Today in many parts of the country local plants offer cement, sulfuric acid, and other commodities — and succeed because their customers come to them for value at an attractive price.

When the availability of the product itself is sufficient to interest buyers, or the availability at a superior price, then this available

117

product strategy is an effective focus level. It brings minimum contact with the customers, no involvement in their business, and marketing costs tend to be lower than for any other approach.

AVAILABLE PRODUCT FAMILY. Here the first rudiments of the marketing concept enter. A producer moves beyond simple production of a basic product, and begins to offer some of the variations which make it fit a broader range of customer needs or preferences. Henry Ford offered the Model T as an available product and then began to build a distribution and service network to support it. But although he refused to consider the consumer desire for other colors than black, he did begin to build variations on the basic sedan design — the coupe, the pickup truck, and so forth. By building a family of products, he broadened the appeal of the Ford product line.

TURNKEY PRODUCTS. Here a manufacturer has decided to reach out to the market and support products in use. Products are not only offered for a specific purpose, but a service force is available to be sure that they work. Singer succeeded with the sewing machine in part because of a network of distributors who would not only sell and service the machine, but would teach the customer how to use it. Marketing costs are increased by this approach, which builds much closer ties to the customer, and in this case sold a great many sewing machines.

A turnkey product is one that the customer buys with the manufacturer's assurance that it will be made to work for that customer. Many complex or technical products require this sort of an approach, but it is expensive. A commitment to this focus strategy is also a commitment to an overhead cost for technical service or other product support, so that the business requirement is that revenues be enough greater than could be obtained otherwise to result in higher profits in spite of the higher cost.

TURNKEY SOLUTIONS. Sometimes a manufacturer takes an aggressive approach towards a specific market, and instead of just selling one line of goods, offers expertise in choosing between competitive types of products, selling the one which may be best for that application. Several glass companies redefined themselves as packaging companies, and began to offer a choice — they would study an application and then recommend and supply glass, aluminum, steel plastic, or cardboard, whichever container would do the job best for the customer.

This approach requires real expertise on the part of the vendor in all of the competitive materials, but can lead to a firm, long-term relationship with a satisfied customer. Extra costs include the technical staff which develops and presents this expertise, and the rearrangement of the business to allow a variety of different product lines to be offered as alternates.

PACKAGED PERFORMANCE. The traditional sales approach for a strong specialty is that of packaged performance. Loctite offered to sell a result, by means of a superior chemical bond — in effect a chemical lock washer — at the same price as a metal lock washer. The customer was to look at the result and pay for it. The nature of the product or what it might cost to make was not a part of the discussion.

A packaged performance approach is only possible where a strong specialty exists, and then only if the product nature and composition need not be disclosed. This approach differs from the turnkey solution approach, because only one product is being offered, rather than a variety and this product is offered for superior results. A packaged performance approach often lends itself to effective marketing — an example was the development of a consumer market for high-strength adhesives started by the KRAZY GLUE television promotions. But such marketing tends to be expensive, so that a packaged performance product needs a large enough margin to cover promotion expense and still return a worthwhile profit.

PACKAGED SERVICE. A packaged service approach to a market is the sale of a result — such as soft water — with the necessary products and services handled together by the vendor for a fee. Xerox had major success promoting some of its copy machines on a packaged service basis — the machine was 'free,' and so were the service and supplies — but there was a charge of a few cents each for the copies. From that few cents each times many millions of copies a major revenue stream was built.

A packaged service approach tends to be expensive, and requires a deep understanding of the consumers' needs. It can often be extremely rewarding if the result which is being sold is not easily duplicated by others.

CRAFTSMANSHIP. Here all sales are on a custom basis. The business is built on the reputation and expertise of the craftsmen, and this leads the customers to ask for work requiring this expertise. Arthur D. Little or any other firm selling research services positions itself in this way, as do many of the major engineering and construction firms, or the companies which do custom chemical synthesis or regulatory approval work. Overheads tend to be high, because the talent must be on hand and there is no routine flow of products to the market generating revenue — only a stream of discrete projects.

Stages And Levels

The seven levels of focus represent seven different types of relationship between a business selling products and services and its customers. No one of these levels is necessarily right or wrong, but they do tend to represent an increasing degree of involvement between the seller and the life or business of the buyer, with increasing overhead costs and increasing possibility of protection from competition. When matched with the four stages of product differentiation, they show the potential for a given strategist to select and develop any one of $4 \times 7 = 28$ different businesses, by combining different stages and levels, as illustrated in Figure 1.

Figure XIV-1			
Levels of Focus versus Stages of Differentiation			
	Unique Product	Strong Specialty	Weak Specialty	Commodity
1 Available Products				
2 Available Product Family				
3 Turnkey Products				
4 Turnkey Solutions				
5 Packaged Performance				
6 Packaged Service				
7 Craftsmanship				

All 28 of these combinations are possible, and businesses with these characteristics can be described and located. Packaged performance and packaged service businesses are most commonly associated with strong specialty products or services — but a packaged service business based on a commodity level of service is the industrial cleaning business, a difficult, labor-intensive, competitive business dependent on taut management of low-skill, high-turnover labor.

More important than the fact that these 28 boxes can be filled with possible businesses are two tests for any strategy which may be under consideration. In the first place, the match between the level of focus and the level of overhead and market support expense that this implies should be factored into the planning early. While there is no doubt that a good technical service force can increase the appeal of a product line in the eyes of the customers, will they be willing to pay enough more to return the extra expense? The chemical industry has accumulated far too many examples of effective technical service of a commodity product — where the customers cheerfully and gratefully use the service and then place their orders where the price is lowest.

Focus planning requires a match of product support as required by the focus level, and leverages on the customer which will secure the extra business the support was intended to generate. But the match is not always possible, and part of the purpose of the planning process is to avoid mistakes such as adding an extra service that will not increase business.

The second utility of focus planning is in the increased understanding of the market relationships which it brings, and the possible application of the insights which this understanding brings to the positioning of the product or service in the market. The four stages of product differentiation originate partly from the customers, and partly from the marketer. Often there are choices within the marketer's control.

It is always possible to shift a product down toward the commodity end of the scale, but few marketers would wish to do this. Sometimes it is possible to shift a product up, toward the specialty end, and this may have a significant impact on strategy. Leavitt[2] has argued that a good marketer can differentiate any product, and certainly there are possibilities that often go unrealized. If the stage of the product and the product support required by the focus do not match — can the product be shifted from commodity at least to a weak specialty level? In most markets a weak specialty can be created, although it may take some development investment.

The Art of Focus

Focus has a purpose, or several purposes. It must pay for itself in the present, from the specific product or service under consideration. Also, it has potential for helping to build the sort of positions which provide future leverages and a continuing profit stream.

A business can go its own way, producing products which customers come and buy, and never be close to its customers or their businesses. Or, a business can get involved in how its customers live or do business, and learn much about new needs and new directions in which the business will turn in the future. Sometimes this extra involvement pays off handsomely, and many of the successful specialty companies depend on it. In other cases the extra information is not worth the extra cost. The art of focus is simultaneously to choose the best match between product or service positioning and focus in the present, and the best strategy for using today's focus and today's success to build positions for the future.

CAP Analysis: What Will The Competition Do?

So far this discussion has emphasized internal consistency of focus and of product and business strategy. Far too many actual planning exercises stop at this point as if there were only one firm trying to get a share of the market. But most businesses and most products have competitors, and they should be considered in the planning also.

CAP analysis deals with competitive action potential. Competitive action potential can be derived rather rapidly by most groups, if they take the time. After all, there are not that many important competitors — most groups can narrow the field rather rapidly to between two and six other firms which are the ones to watch. And these firms are not unknown. Usually the management people, particularly in the marketing area, are acquainted with the managers and aware of the personality of the competitive firm, and some of its strengths and limitations. Given this familiarity, it is the work of only a brief group discussion to develop a profile of what a given competitor is and how that firm is likely to behave.

Then in the planning the group decides on an exciting strategy which will have a major impact on the market. When will each of the competitors learn about this, and what will they do? The 'when' can be guessed by the nature of the trade relationships — does 'everybody' know that a major promotion is in preparation, even though they may not know what the product is? Or will competitors see approval notices, or hear reports on field tests? Most groups can guess rather accurately when their competitors will first hear of a new product or promotion.

What can they do about it? Actually, the number of options a given competitor has are not that large — rarely more than five or six possibilities and usually fewer. And from the profile of the firm, coupled with the impressions of the group, it will be possible to rule out some of these options as unlikely or impossible. For example, if a competitor's plants are already on overtime due to production troubles, that firm will probably not choose a response which requires rapid manufacture of new merchandise — and so forth.

Normally a CAP analysis results in a list of two or three possible responses per competitor for a small number of key firms. This is a small enough number of possible responses for someone to spend a little time thinking about each of them, to see whether any of the competitive actions have the potential for upsetting the planned campaign and whether some slight modification might make the chosen strategy more likely to withstand attack successfully. CAP analysis is a useful tool, and part of a sound product and market planning exercise.

Market Share, Life Cycles, And Other Considerations

Many of the writings on product and market planning emphasize market share, and rightly so. Market share is an important attribute of some very desirable positions. The increased volume may make per unit production, distribution and advertising costs lower, and the cumulative effect of a dominant market presence such as IBM's in the computer market has great value. But market share is a derived variable, not a primary one, and some of the emphasis on market share for its own sake can be misleading. Building strong positions is important, and often this means building market share, but what is important is the result, as measured by the strength and profitability of the business, not who sold the most.

Life cycles were discussed at some length in Chapter VIII, because they are important, and because they should influence product and market planning. That influence comes first in the positioning of the product, which is often related to its stage of growth or maturity, and to its anticipated remaining life, which conditions investment decisions related to it.

The essence of product and market planning is the proper combination of the concepts and tools suggested here and in earlier chapters, and common sense. The foundation is customer need. The product or service must satisfy this need. The customer must be led to choose one firm's product or service over the competitive offerings often enough to keep the business going. To win this choice there must be incentives — leverages and positions based on a planned focus — and the whole plan which results should hang together as a logical, believable package.

FOOTNOTES

[1]George C. Sawyer, Seminar: "Product and Business Strategy," Chicago, Los Angeles, Houston, New York, Toronto, Atlanta, Sponsored by *Chemical Week,* 1980.
[2]Theodore Leavitt, "Marketing Success Through Differentiation — of Anything," *Harvard Business Review,* January/February, 1980, pp 83-91.

CHAPTER XV

EVALUATION OF STRATEGIC ALTERNATIVES

The concept of strategic overview management is as a means to effective strategy formulation, where strategy formulation is the part of the planning process aimed at assuring that the action-laid-out-in-advance is directed at those ends most consistent with the mission and goals of the firm. This chapter will consider how a proposed strategy may be evaluated, to anticipate what its profits and consequences will be, before action is started.

The Strategic Model As A Planning Tool[1]

As a means to maximizing the effectiveness and value added by a planning process, it is useful to construct a simple conceptual model of a proposed strategy for examination and evaluation. Such a model often aids in improving the action plan or in choosing between alternative strategies. It aids in discovery of inconsistent elements in a particular strategy or unexpected consequences of its execution as illustrated in the following examples.

WATCH DISPLAY CHEMICALS. The unexpected offshoot of the fundamental research processes of a multinational corporation was a product and patent position in the chemicals and technology for the visual information displays of digital watches, calculators and instruments. The corporation decided to enter the market as a supplier of these chemicals in the U.S. (and elsewhere).

For this business the mission was that of supplying the display chemical needs of the electronic industry, and among the goals its achievement of a preeminent and profitable market position. The strategy included (I) an ongoing R&D effort to maintain leadership in the rapidly evolving market, (II) initial emphasis on materials needed for watch and calculator displays with products for a wider range of markets to follow, (III) patent protection of the business, insofar as possible, to reinforce the protection already inherent in the technology, (IV) marketing to display manufacturers aimed at develoing an exclusive supply position by offering superior chemical mixtures of a proprietary nature, (V) an attempt to bring the business to a positive cash flow as soon as possible.

While a number of electronic industry, governmental, and other research groups in various countries were actively pursuing improvements in the chemical display technology, no competitor had yet tried to establish a position as the leading chemical supplier to the industry. The existence of the business represented a decision to develop this corporate opportunity after a review of alternatives ranging from abandonment of the patents to direct entry into display, semiconductor and watch manufacture. No corporate social impact problems or needs for course correction were foreseen, in part because the chosen business role affected society only indirectly, through supply of products to consumer products industries. Corporate operations requirements were judged to be well within the established competence of the firm, although this effort was not without its startup problems.

In constructing a strategic model of such a business, the technique is to examine the selected strategy as it must be developed in the light of the technical characteristics and business realities of the effort, to see what the consequences of the strategy must be. These consequences are then examined, to see whether any of them may be undesirable, or suggestive of unsuspected vulnerabilities of the business.

In this case, the analysis would begin with a more detailed consideration of the technology and the product line that it could generate. These were by nature small volume products since a gram of chemical could be made into a large number of watch displays. Because of the complex chemistry, these are high cost products. They also required pricing to give a high gross margin, in order to recover the R&D investment and to have hope of a profit. The initial expectation was of a market which could be developed at a price of $4 per gram in multi-kilo quantities. In the language of Chapter XIV, the firm had chosen a packaged performance approach to the market, based on unique or strong specialty products it hoped to offer.

Chemicals for these displays had extremely high purity requirements but of an unfamiliar type, because they related to electronic industry needs for control of conductivity and electrical characteristics in addition to conventional chemical standards. The product line for this business was conceived as intrinsically small, with a handful of chemical components formulated into proprietary blends tailored to specific application needs.

Product life was expected to be short due to the dynamic nature of the field, with obsolescence probable after about two years. This defined the challenge to R&D, which had the burden of providing the successor products more effectively than competing electronic and chemical laboratories.

The market characteristics suggested that the chemical needs for watches and calculators would support a successful small business, with a growth potential justifying the development largely lying in other and future display applications. Because of the rapid technology shift in the electronic industry, the entire strategy was vulnerable to total replacement of this display technology by a newer one, in the same way that this chemical system had replaced an earlier display chemistry, which itself had replaced light emitting diode displays, all within a few years.

Given the decision to enter the marketplace, a strategic model shows that there were remarkably few managerial choices as to how to proceed. The dynamics of the market and the technology mandated an R&D effort sufficient to renew the line in the face of short product life. Only those few firms able and willing to compete in display and semiconductor technology could be customers. An approach to the market with proprietary mixtures rather than discrete chemical substances gave the only near-term hope of obtaining a large enough share of this small market to make the effort worthwhile. And the entire effort could be supplanted, perhaps in as little as three or four years, if a scientific advance opened the route to development of a superior display technology.

The value of beginning to define this strategy as a strategic model is to discover the tightness by which the course of action was constrained even before entry efforts started. This also permits analysis of the vulnerability or robustness of a strategy against possible disturbances in the chosen environment. In this case the strategy was vulnerable, because management had so little freedom of action within those boundaries if conditions change.

Implementation of this specific strategy started in a promising manner, and then encountered two problems. The most critical was the buying posture of the major electronic companies. They resisted the concept of sole-source suppliers, to the point even of refusing to evaluate product mixtures with superior properties if the composition was proprietary, since this implied dependence on one vendor.

This difficulty was based on bitter experience with chemical and pharmaceutical companies as suppliers which had led the electronic companies to the generalization that any chemical bought from outside would have to be purified anyway, before it would be suitable for electronic industry use. This had caused a number of electronic companies to manufacture their own specialty chemicals in spite of the obvious inefficiencies.

This attitude could be overcome by demonstrating reliable performance and service as a supplier, but at a small initial sales volume based on only a portion of each company's requirements, since policy required a second supplier and most companies continued to make a part of the material for their own use. This also barred all proprietary products and led to a purchasing situation which favored development of price competition.

A second major difficulty in implementing the chosen strategy was the lack of success of the prospective customer group in obtaining their anticipated share of the U.S. consumer market. Unexpectedly, the Japanese and others led in successful innovation, at the expense of established U.S. and European companies. Less market for display chemicals was available in the U.S., and a number of display manufacturers withdrew from the market.

In evaluating the performance of this strategy after about four years, it appeared basically sound and likely to work out in the long run, although greatly delayed by the painful process of developing a reputation for reliability with the electronic companies. Because the strategy had been so tightly constrained from the first, management had no choice but to accept the delay, short of abandonment of the venture. The customers had accepted the products only on a commodity or weak specialty basis, even though the goal still was to move back to selling packaged performance of a strong specialty.

Sales and market growth were proceeding, but far behind original projections. And the U.S. electronic companies, while not competing effectively for watch displays for conventionally-priced watches, had increased their sales volume by enlargement of the market for low-priced watches. Since no new display technology had yet threatened, the investment still had adequate ultimate prospects for profits and return on investment.

In discussing this example, the effort was to bring out of the narrative some of the key elements of a conceptual model of the business strategy being employed. Given a conceptual model, a numerical model also can be considered, but this effort is not justified until some later stage. Here the emphasis is on defining a strategy, developing the framework for its implementation, and examining the consequences as well as the boundaries, the physical limits, the vulnerabilities, and the robustness of the strategy to random events. The purpose is to develop an understanding sufficient so that design of the strategy can be further improved to reduce the chance of misadventure. Quantification can then represent a further refinement of the design, if time permits and the potential increase in precision seems to justify the effort.

Such a conceptual strategic model is built from the mission and goals which provide the strategy its initial validity, modified by the requirements of the strategic overview components. Then the strategy should be identified as to (I) focus of strategy (specialty, commodity, etc. and built on a specific level of involvement with the customer's business), (II) technology, (III) stage of growth of the business, (IV) protection from competitive forces, (V) nature of competitive advantage, (VI) profile of the customer group, and (VII) the technology horizon — when will today's technology be obsoleted, and by what? From this information, the size of the product line and the likely distribution of product sizes, product life, and profitability can be estimated, so that both the likely shape of the business and the nature of the constraints around it begin to emerge more clearly.

SPECIALTY PRODUCTS. As a second example, consider a successful specialty chemical business. This company had taken as its mission the supplying of high performance specialty chemicals from two strong technology positions. It had defined its goals almost entirely in terms of sales and profit growth. Its strategy called for aggressive development of pharmaceutical intermediate plus chemical and electronic industry applications products from these two technologies. The applications development required a strong research and development group, and the company had also taken some R&D contracts, to increase the span of its more fundamental research. Marketing opportunities for its products had been pursued into international markets to an extent unusual for a relatively small firm.

Strategic overview analysis had called for further strengthening of corporate operations, and the gathering of additional resources to hasten the already favorable rate of development of corporate opportunity. No corporate social impact issues had come to light, and potential need for corporate course correction had been minimized.

The competitive advantage of the firm was based on good chemistry and two difficult technologies applied to small markets. The business was young, fast-growing, profitable, and the technology position sound for the foreseeable future. Patents contributed some protection, but largely to the marginal economics rather than the fundamental chemistry of the business. The customer group was defined by the specific applications, with many small single-use products.

The technology made these products expensive and therefore they were used only for superior performance when the needs of an application justified this. The products were priced to be profitable, with long product life in many of the smaller applications. Larger products provided the main hope of significant profits, with the limitation that any product which became large enough to interest a commodity chemical supplier could be preempted and produced by such a company at equal or lower cost. Thus, success of a specific product could lead to the loss of the product, at least as a major source of profit.

This vulnerability to loss of successful products is common among small specialty companies, and, so long as it is recognized, is not a barrier to significant levels of success. In this specific case however, the vulnerability did not seem to have received much attention, even though most of the firm's profits were derived from two excellent products both large enough to be vulnerable to loss. Worse still, the product line contained no intermediate-sized products, where the model of the strategy would require that the product line always contain the potential replacements for any products which might be lost. Thus the development of a strategic model based on the performance of a very attractive and fast-growing business showed a fundamental vulnerability which had not received attention. Action aimed at building intermediate-sized products was strongly recommended, in hopes of maintaining the growth momentum of the firm in the face of predictable product losses.

OTHER TYPES OF BUSINESSES. In other businesses the parameters are different, but modeling works equally well in highlighting them. Thus a commodity chemical business rests on one or another comparative advantage concept for its competitive strengths. This may be a raw materials position, economics of scale in manufacture, market dominance, a patent position, or a geographical limit for a high-weight commodity such as sulfuric acid or cement. But these comparative advantage factors can be identified, analyzed and measured for probable durability against factors such as new technologies, new regulations, inflation, and relative shifts in international currency values. Such a process would be a key part of the strategic model for any commodity business. Comparable models can be constructed for new and old businesses of other types.

SUMMARY: STRATEGIC MODELS. The conceptual strengths of strategic modeling have been suggested here. This is a useful tool for examining, testing and perfecting the strategy of a business: (I) to aid in the choice between alternative strategies, (II) to develop a complete understanding of the chosen strategy, (III) to aid in defining the problems and challenges in its implementation, (IV) to aid in determining whether specific decisions are consonant with a chosen strategy or represent fundamental departures from it. A given strategy has a logical set of consequences; the challenge is to recognize them in advance, as summarized in Figure 1.

Figure XV-I

How To Construct A Strategic Model

I. Define a proposed strategy for a product or business.

II. Characterize the consequences of implementing the strategy, and particulary the evolution of events as the strategy has its impact, sales grow, and competitors respond. Specifically:

A. How will your potential customers and competitors respond to your strategy?
   1. How well do you know your customers?
   2. How sure are you of the way that they will respond?
   3. What are the major options for response from each of your competitors?
   4. Managerially — how much freedom of action do you have to shift your approach once the strategy is in motion? Or, how tightly are you locked in? Can you use extra resources to get extra leverages if you need them?

B. What kind of business are you seeking?
   1. What focus will it require?
   2. What will be its sources of profit, as it succeeds?
   3. What sort of a product line are you building?
      (number of products, distribution by size, distribution by uniqueness, maturity, and market position.)

C. Very approximately — what will the plan for your product or business look like in five years?
   1. Use the plan outline in Chapter II as a checklist — characterize each element, especially the background, environment and functional plans.
   2. Review this rough plan for feasibility, consequences and surprises. (e.g., if your thrust would take you from nothing to $500 million in five years — you might have difficulty in getting the necessary resources or in spending them intelligently and fast enough to support such a strategy).

III. Turn the proposed product or business over and around, and look at it from as many points of view as possible, within practical constraints. Remember that the purpose is not to pick the strategy apart — but to understand it thoroughly, and particularly to avoid the kind of surprises later from which business disasters are born.

IV. Keep the whole process within the boundaries of common sense.

131

In moving from strategy to consequences, a different set of factors will be strategic to each type of business, just as specialty and commodity businesses differed in the previous discussion, and the two specialty chemical examples differed from each other. In more consumer-focused businesses, distribution may be a critical factor, or the consumer interface itself. Or, in some perfume and cosmetic businesses, one strategic element is that combination of product and promotion which leads to the customer's perception of the value of the product.

A conceptual strategic model, then, will be a useful analytical tool if developed from the set of strategic factors appropriate to that business. It will be useful in the line management process of defining strategy, providing that the management has achieved a strategic overview sufficient to permit wise strategic choices. Strategy is a means to planning, of laying action out in advance. Operating management must step outside of its normal set of perceptual barriers in order to formulate strategy successfully, and strategic analysis by means of conceptual strategic models can aid substantially in this process.

Other Comparative Tools

The strategic model concept has been discussed at some length because it is a simple, useful tool based on common sense, which is none-the-less capable of generating very powerful insights as to the nature of a business and the consequences of its strategy. There are many other tools, of which two types will be profiled briefly. These are the comparative rating systems, and the strategy packages.

COMPARATIVE RATING SYSTEMS. Attempts have been made to assign numerical value to each of the attributes of a business strategy and weightings to the relative importance of each, to make it possible to compare strategies by comparing numerical totals. In general, these techniques fail. The value assignments tend to be too subjective to be summarized in this way, and the summation process tends to obscure the details of the differences between strategies, rather than challenging the mind to explore them.

STRATEGY COMPARISON CHECKLIST. One exception to this indictment is a visual profile comparison of strategies by means of a strategy comparison checklist. This checklist has evolved from a "New Product Profile Chart" developed by Harris[2,3] at Monsanto, and expanded[4] to a broader comparison of business and product strategies.

The strategy comparison checklist is a rating system based on criteria selected for this purpose. Against each of these criteria the strategy is rated from − 2 to + 2 and the resulting ratings plotted as a bar graph. By comparison of the graphs of a series of strategies it is immediately obvious where the strategy has been rated as strong and where it takes the business into new areas or has raised questions. The checklist presented here is based on criteria which fall into five areas:

> Business Overview
> Financial Measures
> Production/R&D Measures
> Market Aspects
> Product and Customer Areas

Within these areas the planning group needs to develop a series of criteria appropriate to its business. Figure 2 gives an example of a set of criteria developed for the Business Overview evaluation. These focus on comparison of the fit of the proposed new product or venture with established corporate patterns and strengths, starting with conformity with mission and goals.

In order to make the checklist usable in this format the group must consider the range of possible answers to the questions which these criteria each raise, select from the relevant answers the good and bad extremes, and fit these answers into the rating scale. Thus in Figure 2 the answers to the "Does it fit our mission?" question range from a clear "yes" which is rated at + 2, to a requirement that the mission be changed in order to accommodate the proposed product or venture — this is rated at -2. In the same way the other questions move the evaluation through the chosen check list for the Business Overview, and on into similar checklists for Financial Measures, as shown in Figure 3, Production/R&D Measures in Figure 4, Market Aspects in Figure 5, and Product & Customer Areas in Figure 6.

The result is a list of 48 criteria divided into five groups. Figure 7 shows a Checklist for Strategy Comparison rating sheet, with the 48 criteria summarized briefly next to space for the ratings. Figures 8 and 9 are examples of ratings of actual strategies.

Figure 8 is an evaluation of a proposed entry strategy by an industrial supplier into a low-technology and competitive consumer product area for which it provides the raw materials. The evaluation shows that this project would represent a change in mission and goals plus investment which could not be recovered in case of misadventure, and marketing at customer stages and levels with which this business is now totally unfamiliar.

133

Figure XV-2
Business Overview

	-2	-1	+1	+2
1. Does it fit our mission?				
	must be changed	fits words; not spirit	fits spirit not words	right on target
2. Does it fit our goals?				
	digression	can be rationalized	as well as expected	yes
3. Does it build on our strengths?				
	weakens by dividing	no	in part	yes
4. Is it consonant with our resources?				
	all eggs in one basket	difficult possible	yes - with strain	yes, easily
5. Does it avoid or minimize our weaknesses?				
	increases them	no	in part	yes
6. Within acceptable environmental impact boundary conditions?				
	increases risks	no	in part	yes
7. Based on a stable technology?				
	will change - bad for us	will change- change OK	probably	yes
8. Familiarity with marketing products at this stage?				
	none	some failures	some successes	yes
9. Familiarity with marketing products at this level?				
	none	some failures	some successes	yes
10. Familiarity with marketing to this type of customer?				
	none	some failures	some successes	yes
11. Familiarity with building & managing this type of market franchise?				
	none	some failures	some successes	yes
12. Familiarity with this specific market?				
	none	some failures	some successes	yes
13. Familiarity with the regulatory environment?				
	none	some failures	some successes	yes
14. Ethics & Business Practices - fit with our business pattern?				
	bad	marginal, but fits	legal, but does not fit	OK & fits

Figure XV-3
Financial Measures

	-2	-1	+1	+2
1. Return on investment*	weak	slightly below std.	slightly above std.	high
16. Estimated annual sales*	weak	slightly below std.	slightly above std.	high
17. New dollar (capital + expense) payout*	weak	slightly below std.	slightly above std.	high
18. Use of existing investment	uses needed capacity	uses excess capacity	none	uses idle plant
19. Flexibility/reversibility of investment	little or none	¼ recoverable	½ recoverable	nearly all recoverable
20. Inflation/pricing characteristics	poor pass-thru; high cost rise	poor pass-thru; avg. cost rise	good pass-thru; avg. cost rise	good pass-thru; low cost rise
21. Years to reach estimated sales*	more than 3	2 - 3	1 - 2	1 or less

*Use standards appropriate to your firm

Figure XV-4

Production/R&D Measures

	-2	-1	+1	+2
22. Ease of competitive entry	anyone can enter	most could enter	difficult entry	few have the resources
23. Raw materials availability	limited supply or suppliers	limited - inside company only	freely available	freely - inside company only
24. Process familiarity	new to us	partly new	familiar	one of our strengths
25. R&D staff availibility	hard to hire	not hard to hire	available & competent	superstars available
26. Know-how availability	breaking new ground	new but not strange	new but familiar	one of the strengths
27. Likelihood of successful development	long shot	difficult project	good chance of success	almost routine
28. Patent status	confused	open field	restricted to a few	patent or exclusive
29. Energy or petrochemical cost dependence	high	low	non-petro-chem, low energy	have own petrochem & energy

Figure XV-5

Market Aspects

	-2	-1	+ 1	+ 2
30. Suitability of present sales force	new group needed	need some additions	need some retaining	fits right in
31. Market stability	volatile-price-cuts	unsteady	fairly firm	highly stable
32. Market trend	shrinking	static; mature	growing	new market opening
33. National/international market	int'l; high import pressure	national or regional; some imports	isolated market	inter-national with high exports potential
34. Market development requirements	extensive	some education needed	small	ready customer acceptance
35. Promotional requirements	high	moderate	low	little or none
36. Technical service requirements	high/no loyalty	moderate	none	high, with price protection
37. Cyclical or seasonal demand	highly	moderately	slightly	high stability
38. Potential market position	small with dominant competitors	small with many competitors	large-many competitors	major share

Figure XV-6
Product & Customer Areas

	-2	-1	+ 1	+ 2
39. Similarity to present products	entirely new	somewhat different	somewhat similar	fits in perfectly
40. Effect on present product	replaces	competes somewhat	no effect	will increase sales
41. Marketability to present customers	different group	some present customers	mostly present customers	all present customers
42. Number of potential customers*	too many - costs high	too few - too dependent	a few more or less than we like	the number we like
43. Product competition	severe	significant	1 or 2 somewhat competitive	none
44. Product advantage	higher price same performance & quality	competitive or higher price and p./q.	competitive with p./q. advantage	price p./q. advantage
45. Length of product life	1 - 3 years	3 - 5 years	5 - 10 years	over 10 years
46. Product liability exposure	large and hard to insure	unknown	small & insurable	very small & already insured
47. Customer's business outlook	hard times & shrinking	sound & stable	cutting costs but expanding	high profit rapid growth
48. C.A.P. potential	expect strong response	expect weak response	expect no response	no response possible

*Use standards appropriate to your firm

138

Figure XV-7
Checklist for Strategy Comparison

Business Overview	-2	-1	+1	+2
1. Fits mission				
2. Fits goals				
3. Builds on strengths				
4. Fits resources				
5. Avoids weaknesses				
6. Evir. boundaries				
7. Stable technology				
8. Product stage OK				
9. Product level OK				
10. Customers OK				
11. Franchise OK				
12. Market OK				
13. Regulatory OK				
14. Ethics OK				

Financial Measures
15. Return on investment
16. Sales
17. New $ payout
18. Use existing equipment
19. Investment flexibility
20. Inflation/pricing
21. Yrs. to estimated sales

Production/R&D Meas.
22. Competitive entry . . . .
23. Raw material avail . . . . . .
24. Process familiarity . . . . . .
25. R&D staff avail . . . .
26. Knowhow avail . . . .
27. Chance of success . . . . . .
28. Patent status . . . .
29. Energy/petro. OK . . . .

Market Aspects
30. Suitability-sales force
31. Market stability
32. Market trend
33. National/int'l market
34. Market devel. requirement
35. Promotional requirement
36. Tech service requirement
37. Cyclical/seasonal
38. Potential market position

Product & Customer
39. Simil. to pres. prod. . . . . . .
40. Effect on pres. prod . . . . .
41. Market-pres. cust. . . . .
42. Number-pot. customers . .
43. Product competition . . . . .
44. Product advantage . . . . . .
45. Length-product life . . . . . .
46. Product liabilities . . . .
47. Cust. bus. outlook . . . .
48. C.A.P. potential . . . .

139

Figure XV-8
Forward Integration Entry Strategy

	-2	-1	+1	+2

Business Overview
1. Fits mission . . . .
2. Fits goals . . . .
3. Builds on strengths . . . . .
4. Fits resources . . . .
5. Avoids weaknesses . . . . .
6. Evir. boundaries . . . .
7. Stable technology . . . .
8. Product stage OK . . . .
9. Product level OK . . . .
10. Customers OK . . . .
11. Franchise OK . . . .
12. Market OK . . . .
13. Regulatory OK . . . .
14. Ethics OK . . . .

Financial Measures
15. Return on investment
16. Sales
17. New $ payout
18. Use existing equipment
19. Investment flexibility
20. Inflation/pricing
21. Yrs. to estimated sales

Production/R&D Meas.
22. Competitive entry . . . .
23. Raw material avail . . . . . .
24. Process familiarity . . . . . .
25. R&D staff avail . . . .
26. Knowhow avail . . . .
27. Chance of success . . . . . .
28. Patent status . . . .
29. Energy/petro. OK . . . .

Market Aspects
30. Suitability-sales force
31. Market stability
32. Market trend
33. National/int'l market
34. Market devel. requirement
35. Promotional requirement
36. Tech service requirement
37. Cyclical/seasonal
38. Potential market position

Product & Customer
39. Simil. to pres. prod. . . . . . .
40. Effect on pres. prod . . . . .
41. Market-pres. cust. . . . .
42. Number-pot. customers . .
43. Product competition . . . . .
44. Product advantage . . . . . .
45. Length-product life . . . . . .
46. Product liabilities . . . .
47. Cust. bus. outlook . . . .
48. C.A.P. potential . . . .

140

Figure 9 is an evaluation of a development and marketing strategy proposed to capitalize on a technology breakthrough making possible superior products for one of the company's present major marketplaces. It requires a long and expensive market development process at a time when the business of the customer industry is depressed.

In neither case does the strategy comparison checklist either make or suggest the proper management decision. The purpose of the checklist is to raise flags of approval or of warning, according to how well a proposed new activity fits in with present patterns, strengths and available resources. However, wherever an activity takes a business into new territory, the step should be a conscious one, taken after due consideration, and after adequate preparations have been made to minimize the problems of mastering new knowledge and techniques.

The use of the strategy comparison checklist requires as a preliminary a review of the value systems built into the evaluation. For example, Number 31 in the checklist is Market Stability — a highly stable market is rated +2 and a volatile, price-cutting market is rated -2. While most companies prefer a stable market, some look for volatile situations and try to gain entry. Such a company would reverse these ratings. Similarly, some companies prefer markets requiring high promotion and market development effort or high customer service requirements, and others do not, and they would adapt the rating scales accordingly.

Some marketing companies may not really care how a proposed strategy is affected by energy or petrochemical costs — if so, then criterion 29 should be discarded as irrelevant. But there may be other criteria important to a given management which should be added. With some thoughtful revision almost any group can adapt the checklist to its own use.

The use of the checklist is as a flagging system, to warn of new areas or new requirements needing specific attention. This helps to avoid a major and frequent strategic error, where a commitment is made to a new activity without fully realizing what the requirements for success are — and then management must reappraise in the light of initial setbacks, and decide whether to increase the effort and investment or to write off the effort.

In no way is this checklist intended to discourage moves into new areas, revision of corporate missions and goals, or major shifts in resources. However in every case such steps should be made with full understanding of implications and cost, and when a given entry strategy requires success in a great many new areas and the overcoming of a multitude of difficulties, as does the entry strategy pro-

Figure XV-9
Technology Breakthrough Development Strategy

	-2	-1	+1	+2

Business Overview
1. Fits mission . . . .
2. Fits goals . . . .
3. Builds on strengths . . . . .
4. Fits resources . . . .
5. Avoids weaknesses . . . . .
6. Evir. boundaries . . . .
7. Stable technology . . . .
8. Product stage OK . . . .
9. Product level OK . . . .
10. Customers OK . . . .
11. Franchise OK . . . .
12. Market OK . . . .
13. Regulatory OK . . . .
14. Ethics OK . . . .

Financial Measures
15. Return on investment
16. Sales
17. New $ payout
18. Use existing equipment
19. Investment flexibility
20. Inflation/pricing
21. Yrs. to estimated sales

Production/R&D Meas.
22. Competitive entry . . . .
23. Raw material avail . . . . . .
24. Process familiarity . . . . . .
25. R&D staff avail . . . .
26. Knowhow avail . . . .
27. Chance of success . . . . . .
28. Patent status . . . .
29. Energy/petro. OK . . . .

Market Aspects
30. Suitability-sales force
31. Market stability
32. Market trend
33. National/int'l market
34. Market devel. requirement
35. Promotional requirement
36. Tech service requirement
37. Cyclical/seasonal
38. Potential market position

Product & Customer
39. Simil. to pres. prod . . . . . .
40. Effect on pres. prod . . . . .
41. Market-pres. cust. . . . .
42. Number-pot. customers . .
43. Product competition . . . . .
44. Product advantage . . . . . .
45. Length-product life . . . . . .
46. Product liabilities . . . .
47. Cust. bus. outlook . . . .
48. C.A.P. potential . . . .

142

filed in Figure 8, management should certainly look for far-above-average profit prospects, to justify the extent of the exposure.

STRATEGY PACKAGES. What are here called strategy packages have also been called packaged strategic planning processes; the reference is to standardized approaches to solving all strategy problems, as have been offered by many consulting groups. Some deal with product and business strategy, some with resource strategy, and some with both. The General Electric portfolio approach to managing resource strategy is an example, although this was developed internally by GE for its own use. Given the GE value systems and the assigned rules for comparison, application of these rules will produce a rating suggesting whether a given strategy or business should be accepted or discarded.

These strategy packages are widely applied and are probably of net value to the companies applying them, although there is an undercurrent of concern as to whether a cookbook application of a 'canned' strategy package may sometimes cause major blunders, if client companies encounter conditions beyond the range of the simplifying assumptions on which such approaches tend to be built.

The theme here is intended to be one of caution. Careful evaluation of these strategy packages — or packaged strategic planning processes — is needed, and Goldenberg[5] is developing comparative tools, and an attempt to get a broad-based evaluation of the strengths and weaknesses of the major packages is just getting under way.

Strategy Evaluation

A strategy is such a central element of a business or of any organization, that mistakes in strategy hurt very badly. Thus caution is in order before a strategy is put into action. This is common sense, much like looking to see where a gun is pointed before pulling the trigger.

Careful evaluation is wise, before a strategy is applied, but sometimes time presses and action cannot be postponed. The strategic model discussed above is a broad, common sense approach and widely applicable. For some purposes the strategy comparison checklist is also very useful. The various strategy packages are being widely used also, and are good within the limits of their underlying assumptions — but too often these limits are unclear or unknown.

Whatever technique is used — consider carefully, but quickly, before committing your organization's resources and yourself to a particular strategy.

FOOTNOTES

[1]Adapted and expanded from George C. Sawyer, "The Use Of Strategic Models In Setting Goals," *MSU Business Topics,* August, 1979, pp. 37-44.

[2]John S. Harris, "New Product Profile Chart," *Chemical & Engineering News,* April 11, 1961, pp 110-118

[3]John S. Harris, "New Product Profile Chart," *Chemtech,* September 1976, pp 554-564.

[4]George C. Sawyer, Seminar: "Product and Business Strategy," Chicago, Los Angeles, Houston, New York, Atlanta, Toronto; sponsored by *Chemical Week,* 1980.

[5]David I. Goldenberg and George C. Sawyer, forthcoming in *Planning Review.*

CHAPTER XVI

PLANNING, AND FORMAL
PLANNING SYSTEMS

In any organization with more than two or three managers, as they share in the planning, the vehicle through which their joint plans for action get laid out is a planning system of some sort. Planning in organizations tends to lead to formal planning systems, but formal systems are only a means to an end — they do not cause planning to occur, and can even prevent it, when their emphasis is too much on form instead of substance.

The general question to which this chapter is devoted is that of how an organization designs or evolves an effective planning system, or how it may judge the effectiveness and efficiency of the system it already has. The answer starts with the general principles of planning, and the broad approach to the facilitation of the line management planning process, but cannot narrow to any one specific formula for the way that a business enterprise or other organization should plan. It cannot and should not come down to a specific formula because the planning system — as a key element in the management operating system of the firm — is a part of the nervous system of that enterprise, to use the biological analogy.

The nervous system of that enterprise is a very intimate and personal reflection of the kind of business it is, the kind of people who manage it, and the kind of environment that they manage in. Different firms differ radically in these dimensions, and to serve management's needs the management operating system and the planning system must differ correspondingly from firm to firm.

What Should Be The Nature Of The Planning System?

Among the determinants of the nature of the planning system are the goals and strategy of the management collectively, and of the managers as individuals. As discussed earlier, a business needs a defined mission, a set of goals whose accomplishment would represent progress towards fulfilling the mission, and a strategy aimed at achieving these goals. And as the strategy of the enterprise varies, the sort of planning system which will serve it best will change.

Thus General Motors, which has demonstrated its ability to achieve market leadership in a host of related engine-product businesses ranging from cars and trucks to school buses and diesel locomotives, attempted to use its World War II experience in building aircraft engines as the foundation of a permanent position in this type of engine product — and failed.

Drucker has ascribed this failure to a failure to adapt the corporate system and thinking to the requirements of a very different business. Where the other General Motors businesses had approximately the same product development cycle and similar new product management characteristics, aircraft engines are developed on a far longer cycle and the business has different management characteristics. The General Motors management operating system and planning system were geared to the planning requirements of a series of engine-product markets with rather similar planning and management characteristics. The strategies for success in the aircraft engine market required a different planning and management system. General Motors failed to perceive this clearly enough to adapt, and eventually withdrew from this business.

The personal goals and strategy of the management group influence the type of planning system also. No management group is able to accept all challenges equally well — most of the better managements restrict themselves to certain tasks and challenges they feel well able to handle. While this can cause their enterprises to miss potential opportunities, the cost of failures is high. An ambitious management which succeeds in most of its undertakings is highly prized and not that common, to the point that it is unlikely to be criticized for not undertaking still other new ventures at which it might have failed.

But this means that management, in focusing on opportunities it feels well able to handle, will also be selecting business areas it likes, and influencing the design of the business by its own desires and preferences. If the profits are high, who will complain if a highly profitable New York business successfully extends its territory first to Florida rather than California because the executives prefer to travel there?

As the preferences of the executive group influence the evolution of the business, they will tend to provide a gentle additional constraint, so that some areas within the corporate mission and goals and consonant with its chosen strategy will be developed before others. This extra constraint should be reflected also in the design of the planning system, and recognized rather than hidden — in part because the distinction between proper choice of areas where management is most likely to succeed, and capricious direction of the corporate effort for personal reasons can be a subtle one, and the subtlety is most easily managed in the open.

Another major influence on the design of the management operating system and of the planning system is the corporate culture. A corporation or any other organization acquires its own life-force and identity as soon as it begins to function — initially based on the personalities of its members and the style and manner in which management manages it. Then as time passes these habits of operation become more and more deeply ingrained, and new managers often find it easier to fit into the established operating pattern than to change it. This pattern becomes a constraint, even on the chief executive, who will often carry on traditions, particularly awards and ceremonies, which he or she would never have initiated — because "it has always been done that way." A major organization acquires a tradition and a history, and many of its members cherish and work to preserve these traditions.

These preexisting patterns which even the top management rarely attempts to change are also constraints on the planning system. An organization which has had a paternal, hierarchical autocratic tradition is likely to move much more slowly into a broadly based, participative planning system design than another organization with informal and more democratic operating traditions.

The planning system is an assistance to a line management planning process. The design of the system should vary according to the way in which the management can most effectively carry out this planning. The abilities of the members of the management group, their backgrounds, the organizational and personal goals and strategies, and the kind of a corporate tradition and culture in which they function are all constraints to the design. There is no optimum planning system design, except that design which aids a particular management of a specific business to manage most effectively.

Choosing The Starting Point For Planning

A plan is the product of a process. The important thing in most real-world planning staff assignments is to improve the flow of this process — to identify it, to bring it to the surface, to cause it to interact with the management aspirations for the evolution of the business or business operation. A critical element in helping a group of managers with their first formal plan is to choose a starting point appropriate to the situation and the purpose — from an analysis of the heritage and inertia of the planning process as it exists, since a planning process always does exist in an ongoing operation. Equally important is the engagement with the rest of the management operating system in that area. The need is to establish a credible relationship rapidly and then to build from this entry into the planning, and toward the kind of a planning process most useful to the management of that area.

ANALYZING THE ONGOING PLANNING SYSTEM. Choice of a starting point for a planning effort is a matter of judgment to be tempered by an understanding that such a start is in fact a diversion or enlargement of a process already underway. Wherever a unit is being managed, its work is being planned in one way or another. The recurrent cycle which represents the planning process is already in progress, and it represents the familiar if imperfect way to plan. "Startup of planning" is a misnomer that tends to put down the efforts of those who have already managed successfully, no matter how urgent it may be to establish more effective planning.

Rather, the role is one of analyzing and understanding enough about the ongoing planning process to decide how best to influence its course; whether to join in this process and reinforce it, or to reshape it by a challenge of one sort or another. The purpose is to move towards an objective in terms of planning performance at the rate required by the circumstances, but with a minimum of unnecessary disruption of the flow of the management operating system.

Where the organization can move in an orderly way over a span of two or three years, the logic would be for those charged with the planning function smoothly to join with the planning process as it exists, to attempt to aid each individual manager in solving perceived planning problems, and indirectly to influence an improvement in effectiveness of this component of management skills. This approach can be very effective because the interaction between the planning problems of different managers tends to mean that each improvement in planning by one manager sets higher standards for the others.

With a skillful planning function a significant fraction of the organization's problems can begin to surface and to be addressed more openly and more effectively than in the past. But this approach takes time and in some cases it may be necessary to confront problems more rapidly, even though this is more traumatic for the organization and requires a much higher level of direct support from top management.

THE PLANNING SYSTEM AS IT EXISTS. In studying the existing planning system, perhaps the key element is the degree to which this system is a conscious or even a programmed part of the corporate process, versus a personal or even intuitive process of individual managers. In order somewhat to categorize the range of possible situations, the existing planning situation can be classified as (I) virgin, (II) a partially established system, (III) established and sound system, (IV) operating but unsound system, (V) planning system discredited and abandoned.

A virgin planning situation is one where no serious effort at formalizing or integrating the planning of the managers has been attempted. Here the missionary work of selling the concepts remains to be done, and the necessary teaching and support as various techniques are first attempted, but there is no negative heritage of mistakes and failures to be overcome.

A partially established planning system represents a beginning, with some of the work done and some of the mistakes made. A new effort must be keyed into the old effort if the value of the start is to be preserved, and the nature and extent of past problems must be surveyed in order to deal intelligently with the problems such failures create.

A sound, established planning system represents a startup problem only when new techniques or new people are being brought into the system, or when management is placing new requirements on it. Or perhaps the approach needs to be varied, to keep the planning effort streamlined, relevant to the business problems, and useful to management. But such a system also has its heritage from past good and bad experiences, and this heritage conditions its reaction to changes.

A planning system that is well accepted but defective is a particularly difficult challenge. Such a situation arises when plans are built on superficial assumptions, and may last until the weaknesses of these assumptions becomes obvious. It is not rare to find erroneous definition of markets, customer behavior, price sensitivity or competitive position woven into a strategy or plan. Before the defect causes a business disaster or discredits the planning effort entirely, its identification and correction may be difficult.

Such an operating but unsound planning system represents

one of the most difficult situations. This is also the case where plans that have no substance or impact are being written and submitted because their writing has become required as a part of an annual procedure. This pursuit of form without substance is a total waste and diversion of resources. It implies a total lack of management interest in the substance of planning, and makes it doubly difficult to stir interest in that substance at any level.

An organization in which formal planning has failed and been abandoned is a difficult one to enter also, but in many ways less difficult than the preceding case in which the failure has not been abandoned. Careful assessment of the reasons the system went astray is useful to the planning function, as well as an understanding of the specific nature of the scars and misconceptions the failure has left behind it.

APPRAISING THE LEGACY. Besides considering the operating status and level of acceptance of the existing planning system, several other dimensions deserve attention. The entire climate is set by the state of health of the underlying business, by the urgency of the decision problems that are seen to press upon it, and by the practical necessity for the planning staff to obtain organizational support for any particular course of action. Other parts of the heritage from the past include the conceptual strengths and weaknesses of the types of planning that the managers are employing, the degree of formality or informality with which planning has become invested, and the levels of acceptance and credibility of the results of the planning at various management levels. Underlying all of this is the question of the degree and variability of top management support for building and maintaining planning as a component of management activity.

THE PROBLEM OF SYSTEM ENTRY. A planning system is running; otherwise the organization would not be functioning. What is spoken of as the startup of a new planning effort is not a startup at all, but a choice of a point, a time and an approach to system entry that will allow appropriate, effective influence, redirection or replacement of the existing planning effort with one that now and continually adapts, the better to serve the changing needs of the managers whose planning the system embodies and assists.

Entry requires a starting point, which should be selected with some care. The energy for the entry may come from a management directive and demand, or may be left for the planning staff to capture by tapping into the energy flows in the management operating system.

Mechanical Factors In Planning System Design

HOW LONG IS A PLAN? One of the first questions for any new planning effort is "how long?" The answer is complex. In theory, any plan should deal with the full futurity of its decisions, and this differs from business to business. A consumer products marketing business may have a new product design and development cycle of less than a year from first concept to full-scale marketing, and may find that a three-year plan takes them farther into the long range than their sales and product management groups are accustomed to think.

Yet businesses with heavy capital investment, positions in high technology, or long and elaborate regulatory processes must deal with tremendous spans of time in order to see projects to completion, before the operation and payback really starts. Some of the nuclear power projects still under construction seem to have originated at a planning stage at least twenty years ago. And investments in basic research, whether in electron physics at Bell Laboratories or in one of the pharmaceutical research institutes, will be many years even in moving to the point of specific product applications.

For a great many businesses the futurity of the decisions the management must make is greater than the span for which it has the tools to plan adequately, and most planning systems are based on shorter cycles which, if carefully conceived and articulated, can serve as a basis for long-term studies quite adequately also. The way this works is for the business to choose a basic time horizon for its planning which serves near-term needs for detail and which does not go so far into the future as to strain the forecasting tools available.

Many organizations have settled on a five-year planning horizon, based on these considerations, and a smaller number extend this basic plan farther in the future, perhaps to ten years. A five year plan is not by itself adequate for a business whose major decisions have a fifteen or more year futurity, but it does provide a clear starting point. Then, using this five-year plan as a basis, narrower and more limited projections for specific components of the business can be made for fifteen years, or for fifty years, as may be appropriate.

One major multinational with a five-year long-range planning cycle regularly does a fifteen year plan for its world-wide needs for production capacity for major product lines. This fifteen year horizon allows enough lead time for a major process development effort preceding the next new plant investment, if changes in technology make this appropriate. This is not a business plan, and does not deal with what the product prices will be or whether the product line will be making money fifteen years in the future — it assumes the need to produce for a growing market and works out the best way to do it.

This sort of a limited functional plan is an excellent way to deal with one component of the business by itself, but dangerous if it must deal with the business as a whole or changes in strategy.

PLANNING CYCLES. Another detail, but of very great importance, is the choice of a time pattern for the planning effort. Most organizations review and revise their plans every year, because this keeps the plan more or less current with the flow of events, although a smaller number postpone revisions until the previous plan is clearly obsolete.

The time of year for annual plan revision can vary with the relationship between the plan and the other elements in the management operating system. For example, some managements want a tight integration of plans and budgets. These may schedule to complete planning for the long-range and for the next year at the same time, and then approve the first year of the long-range plan as the budget for the next fiscal year. This system has many advantages, but it causes a work peak, in that management must consider both long-range and short-range issues at the same time, and strategic issues may sometimes be neglected.

Other organizations, in order to spread out the staff work as well as the demand on management time, put the consideration of long-range and strategic issues off-cycle with the budgets. Thus a corporation which budgets in the fall for a fiscal year starting January 1 may do its strategic and long-range planning in the spring.

This allows a less hurried consideration of the strategic overview issues and of necessary changes in business strategy, and yields an approved plan in the general shape of the next budget either by early summer or early fall, depending on the revisions necessary to get management approval of the plan. It should then be relatively easy to turn this plan into a budget in the fall, and management should know in advance about how the budget will look. That is the theory, and it works well enough to ease the pain of budget time, most of the time.

These two cycles are the most common patterns, but there are many variations — full planning and budgeting in the fall but with separate consideration of isolated strategic issues in the spring — full-scale and exhaustive reviews of individual businesses at a time separate from the rest of the planning — these are only a few of many examples. The key is not the specific pattern, but a planned pattern both of planning system demands on organizational time, and of planning system interaction with the top management decision process, so designed as to help the planning system to add value beyond its cost, as measured by its impact on management decisions and actions.

COMPUTER MODELS AND COMPUTER SUPPORT. Most planning activities will make some use of computer support and of computer models, and several potential applications have been mentioned in earlier chapters. Computer time-sharing services plus software and hardware vendors will provide literature and demonstrations to any potential customer. For those not already familiar with this area, Naylor's book provides a good starting point[1], so that only two related points need to be added here.

The first is the justification — in having the conveniently available summary, analytical and manipulative power which well-chosen computer tools can provide — so that a planning function which does not make appropriate application of such tools is missing a significant opportunity to increase its own effectiveness.

The second point is that of purpose, versus the choice between powerful computer tools of different sorts. A major difficulty of those not familiar with this area is that of applying good tools for the wrong purpose, thus reducing the effectiveness of the effort.

For example, many available programs now will accept the financial data for specific business units and produce from this a consolidation to a group or corporate total. This is a very simple capability yielding reports like those the accounting group has been producing for many years, but can have significant value as a base for testing variations and alternatives as planning progresses.

This is not nearly so powerful or versatile a capability as a simulation which models the variables in the income statement as a series of simultaneous equations and projects the impact of market, economic or other variables on the evolution of the business. But modeling tends to have one purpose, and simple aggregation of data has another, and the choice between the two is more a function of this purpose than of the differing power of the two approaches.

Modeling tends to help a planning function to understand the business system and how to advise management on the manipulation and control of this system. Simple aggregation tends to be more useful in planning itself.

The difference is that, as the actual planning of line management proceeds, the managers tend to need involvement with the choices as the planning proceeds. They get this involvement by looking at the statements of relationship between a driving variable such as disposable income or rate of sales increase in the customer industry, and by handling the numbers that determine how these variables will affect the plan.

This is not efficient, in a rate-of-estimating results sense, but it is effective, in a getting-plans-we-believe-in sense. That is, while a computer simulation could produce a given output estimate faster and better without a group of executives making the translation between external and internal variables, a viable plan can only arise if those executives fully understand what the projected results mean and where they came from. Too often a computer simulation is so powerful that the managers really have no idea where the numbers came from — they can either accept the computer output on the basis of blind faith, or not really accept it at all. Often when a plan founders for lack of support of the managers who must implement it, one of the causes is lingering uncertainty in their minds as to what the plan really means or how its outputs were calculated.

Therefore, in planning the computer support of given planning system a wise course is to focus first on using the power of simulation only as an aid to the staff, with only straightforward aggregative tools used to aid the line planning process. Later it should be possible to increase the power and complexity of the tools used in the line planning process as the level of understanding of computer processes amongst line management rises — but it would be false progress to upgrade too fast and lose the executive involvement and understanding upon which the commitment to the resulting plans must be based.

Fitting In The Planning System

The organization functions through a management operating system which has the planning system as an important component part. Corollary to the need to allow for the time demands imposed by the planning system on the managers and on the staffs is a need to relate the planning system to the other elements in the management operating system.

This is common sense, that all parts of the system should function in a mutually beneficial way, so that they can make the greatest positive contribution to the organization. But common sense does not always get applied unless management insists on it, in the corporate world of departments with jealousies and limited perception of the total corporate need. Sometimes a special effort has to be made to fit these corporate efforts together into an efficient whole, and the planning function, having the broader perspective, often must take the lead in working out inter-departmental accommodations so that the different parts of the management operating system do not interfere with each other as they function.

The purpose, of course, is a maximum-effective effort — one where the ratio between its cost, including management time, and the improvement in the quality of management decisions which results from the planning effort is as favorable as possible. While the details will differ from organization to organization, one of the characteristics of a maximum-effective planning effort is the minimum-possible level of formality and procedure.

The reasons that planning systems sometimes have elaborate procedures and generate ponderous written documents are rooted in the nature of the communication processes in large organizations, which require detailed written statements widely circulated, and so forth. But this formality adds nothing else, and it has high costs.

People have a habit of creating more forms and procedures than necessary, and of holding on to familiar reports and routines even when they no longer have a purpose. But these formalities have two heavy costs — first the direct cost of keeping, circulating, reading and storing the results, and second the larger penalty as the organization loses flexibility and the ability to respond to opportunity or threat, because it is so involved in its own procedures.

The design for the best planning system is the simplest, least cumbersome system which will contribute effectively to the line management planning process of that organization, to make the action-laid-out-in-advance component of the management operating system as potent and competitively effective as the talents of the management group and the available resources can make possible.

FOOTNOTES

[1]Thomas H. Naylor, *Corporate Planning Models*, Addison-Wesley, Boston, 1979.

CHAPTER XVII

PLANNING AND THE ROLE OF THE PLANNING FUNCTION

Planning is a line management task. It is a line management task because, as action-laid-out-in-advance, planning can only be carried out by someone with the line authority to lay out action, commit to its execution, and follow through to fulfill this commitment.

As mentioned earlier, this leaves the planning function and the planning director in a somewhat anomalous position, because they would seem to have a planning assignment and role, but the preceding definition largely bars them from doing planning directly. The work of Planning is primarily not planning, but a mixture of other things related to helping the line management planning process to function at the maximum level of effectiveness the experience and ability of the managers will permit. This chapter is devoted to a discussion of some of the things that the planning group does, as it pursues the tasks necessary for its function.

Roles Of The Planning Function

The members of the planning staff or others assigned to the planning function must be prepared to act in a variety of different roles within the organization, and must be able to keep the duties and responsibilities of these different roles clear and separate, if they are to be viable and productive in their function.

Most staffs function as simple extensions of the function of their executive superior. This gives a clear line of reporting responsibility, organizational loyalty and communication. It is automatically assumed, for example, that if any member of the quality control staff or of the plant security force becomes aware of a violation of procedures, that this awareness will be quickly communicated to organizational superiors — and no member of another department is likely to tell a member of either staff about procedures violations unless they should be so communicated.

But the planning function is different. Because of the way in which an effective member of the planning group assists various line executives, that individual becomes aware of a variety of details which are otherwise confidential within the operating unit — and if these confidences are not respected, that individual is no longer permitted the access necessary to perform planning-support functions. To make this clearer, some of the variety of roles in which planning staffs normally function will be listed and described.

CONSULTANT. Planning staff members or others charged with the planning function frequently find themselves acting as consultants to other staffs and to line managers. Consulting is a private advisory role in which the first allegiance, within reasonable bounds of discretion, is to the client; the task is to aid that client in accomplishing his or her objectives. This contrasts with a normal staff role where the primary allegiance is to the manager or executive group to which the staff reports.

The more normal staff task is often to complete an analysis or a project for some member of the executive group, and the staff member goes about the organization on a mission identified or shielded by the name of that executive. But a consulting task is more client-private, in that the manager must have some degree of trust in the consultant before allowing access to the information which permits that help to be effective. Where a group divides its energies between staff and consulting activities, as planning departments often do, great discretion is needed in the staff assignments in handling information gained from consulting relationships.

While the direct superior often needs to know some of the details of what is going on, such reporting must be guarded, and the planning director or other head of the unit must take great pains not to use any information the staff has gained through its consulting in a way which would destroy these relationships.

While the major role shift is between consulting and normal staff activities, there are a wide variety of other common roles which planning staff members must sometimes assume. Some of these roles are as facilitator, integrator, scribe, mediator, advocate, negotiator, communicator, counsellor, conscience, director, leader, evaluator, analyst, diagnostician, problem-solver, innovator, entrepreneur, initiator, instructor, documentor, architect of the future, and planner.

The need for and importance of these various roles differs a great deal from organization to organization, and from circumstance to circumstance. The individual with planning function responsibilities should understand the potential of these various roles, and attempt to act in those appropriate to the needs of the planning process, as discussed below.

158

FACILITATOR. A capable member of the planning function will become an expert in organizational protocol and procedure, and while the various members of the organization each have their own channels for expediting and cutting red tape, the planning representative will become a considerable resource whenever the problems are outside of the normal operating contacts of the line. For the fastest way to get a report from some other staff, or to move forward the various elements of the planning process and its inevitable formalities, he or she will be the one who knows how to get things done quickly.

INTEGRATOR. As a gatherer and interpreter of data, the planning function member should become very able at finding the relationships between one element of the organization and the others, helping with their definition, and helping each to understand how the efforts can best be integrated for maximum effectiveness.

SCRIBE. Very often as a group struggles with its planning, the planning manager or other planning representative will find himself or herself in the role of scribe — the one who tries to put these ideas on paper. Support through this role is often one of the most effective staff techniques, since line executives may have difficulty in quickly grasping the concepts behind their goals and strategies — but if someone puts down what these concepts appear to be, such a manager may find it easy to engage with the issues, to shape and polish, to the point that a rough draft can be rapidly converted into a statement of the manager's goals, strategies and beliefs.

Also, when a manager is not quite convinced that it is worth the time to rework the unit's plans and strategies, the planning member sometimes can draft a statement based on the assumption that present plans will not be changed, simply for the purpose of bringing home to the manager in an informal way that the situation is more serious than it at first may have seemed.

Being scribe to the group is hard work, and temporary, but a very effective way to get started. In the long run the scribe role should be shifted, perhaps to a junior member of the operating unit, as a part of the training of any group to be more and more self-sufficient in its planning — especially since this frees the planning member from some drudgery, and the freed time can be applied to upgrading of the planning effort in another way.

MEDIATOR. As an outside member of an operating group struggling with its planning, the planning member will learn about many issues and controversies with other units. Very often these invite mediation, since a misunderstanding or a minor problem between two lower-level people may tend to discredit both of the areas involved if it comes to the attention of the higher levels of management. So the planning member, simply by pointing out that the completion of the plan will bring the issue to the surface, often creates the climate where mediation is easy and the problem disappears before anyone needs to be told about it.

ADVOCATE. As a member of the planning function gets drawn into the details of the operation whose planning he or she is trying to assist, there is an automatic tendency to identify with the aspirations of that group. Further, as the group recognizes the central position and potential role of the planning function, there is often a request for assistance as an advocate, to speak for the group or to help it tell its story to a particular executive whose approvals are needed, or otherwise to make maximum use of any assistance the planning representative or his or her superior could render in moving proposals and projects through the organization.

This is a constructive role, for the planning member to help the group to tell its story and to get necessary approvals, so long as that representative recognizes the responsibilities of that advocate role, and does not let him or herself, or the planning function, be associated with any project which should not be approved or which is being presented without a forthright statement of all of the facts.

NEGOTIATOR. Whenever issues must be negotiated, this creates the potential for using a third party in hopes of getting a better resolution. Many negotiations are too far afield from the normal range of planning function interests, and the negotiator role is less common than some of the others.

However, when a planning representative attempts to mediate an issue between different operating areas, as discussed above, sometimes this uncovers more basic problems where the interests of the two units conflict and a boundary needs to be established. Then the conditions which made mediation possible as discussed above also make negotiation more attractive than an appeal to upper management, and the planning representative is often one of the logical negotiators.

COMMUNICATOR. A large part of the task of any planning function is to carry information and to communicate it. Even though a memo may have spelled out the procedure, the personal description makes it more real and fills in details.

160

Because Planning is central and has a good information flow from most parts of the corporation, its members may be able to supply background to help managers to understand why certain things are being changed.

Some corporations take this natural communicator role and expand it. After the management has approved the plan for the coming year, Planning may be given the task of presenting it to different management groups within the corporation, edited as appropriate, showing them the plan and providing background on strategy changes or shifts in emphasis. In major multinationals, this 'road show' presentation of the corporate plan may go from country to country, as a part of a program to keep the managers in each area both informed and personally involved with the central concerns of the corporation.

Such presentations do not replace the normal and proper flow of information down through the organizational hierarchy, and instructions to the line should never be conveyed in this way — this is only a communication from a key staff. But since Planning is very close to both the planning and the strategy formulation processes of management, it is a logical choice to help communicate to the rest of the managers in the organization the parts of these plans and strategies they need to know.

COUNSELLOR. As a member of the planning function develops good working relationships and becomes a trusted consultant to a manager, a counsellor relationship also may develop. Line management can be a very lonely job, because the people around a given manager each have organizational roles and competitive interests. Often of the people who know enough about the functioning of a business to discuss it, the assigned member of the planning function is the only one 'neutral' enough in an organizational sense so that the manager will venture into discussion of personal and career-related business decisions. Thus the member of the planning function may find him or herself being asked for judgment and advice on very sensitive issues — being asked to give good counsel, in areas where very great wisdom and judgment is needed.

Clearly this is sensitive territory. The staff member will wish to be helpful, but must be very cautious not to attempt advice he or she is not qualified to offer. Fortunately, just the neutral role of reflecting and restating issues is often sufficient. Often the manager can be assisted in this way without the staff member attempting to advise a specific course of action.

CONSCIENCE. The role of conscience is an often unwelcome role the representative from Planning will find it necessary to assume from time to time. Sometimes when an operating group has got into a problem and nobody knows about it, the planning representative learns of it in the course of a discussion. The conscience role is to say "Look, wouldn't it be a good idea if you told your boss about this? Because the controller's staff is going to notice any day, and you know what will happen if they tell him before you do." The planning representative is in an awkward position because to make any direct report would violate the consultant relationship, and not to say anything is to share a degree of responsibility for the problem. The first compromise is the conscience role, to try to get the problem to surface through proper channels.

DIRECTOR. Often a planning representative will be given charge of a project or a task force, and will direct the work of those involved in its completion. This is one of the few roles in which a staff member can move openly to action and accomplishment, as a line manager would.

LEADER. More often than the director assignment, a member of the planning unit may find him or herself as the leader of a group attempting to accomplish something specific. This can be the embodiment of an advocate role — for instance, to begin to attempt to convince a group that a procedure should be changed or a cost allocation shifted — an advocate role with the planning representative leading the group proposing the change.

EVALUATOR. A frequent and pivotal role of Planning is the role of the evaluator. As plans and strategies are being put together, the data flows by and information accumulates. Someone — it should be everyone — should be watching the pattern as the information builds, to point out to the group when the facts begin to support — or rebut — the position that they advocate. This is a natural role for a member of the planning function.

ANALYST. A planning representative needs the analytical skills and ability to use analytical tools which help to find patterns in the relevant and irrelevant information in which a problem or issue is bathed. Continually he or she should be analyzing the data. In part this will form the basis for the evaluations cited above.

DIAGNOSTICIAN. Perhaps this is included in the scope of any good analyst, but it is so important that it is worth stating separately as a separate role. As a business plan takes shape, or information flows to any other problem, beyond the ability to analyze the data, find relationships, and evaluate the results, is the rare skill of understanding what is really driving these events and which are truly the controlling variables. Those who are really good at this level of diagnosis are invaluable in their contribution to any complex business planning process.

PROBLEM—SOLVER. Beyond knowing what the problem is, some people are better than others at figuring out what to do about it. Another highly desirable characteristic for a planning function member is the ability to see simple and direct solutions to problems. Where this role is well performed it increases the Planning contribution markedly.

INNOVATOR. An innovation is a useful new combination of resources. In any planning process a major part of the emphasis is on the best possible combination of the available resources, so that the innovation rate in productive planning work is quite high. While the planning representative is not a planner, in the sense of not being able to define and accomplish new resource combinations for the business, very often he or she can aid the group materially in finding such new contributions. Although the credit for new ideas usually goes to the line — as a part of the practical politics of an effective planning unit, and because the line puts the ideas into practice and realizes the innovation — behind the scenes the planning representative can be very effective and contribute substantially to innovation in this way.

ENTREPRENEUR. Occasionally a member of the planning function is put in charge of a business project which will not fit anywhere else in the organization, or that no other group wants, and is put in the role of entrepreneur. Some organizations go farther in encouraging this sort of activity, even to the point of a related venture capital or new ventures group. While the role of entrepreneur is one many planning function members never assume, many others do face this opportunity and challenge.

INITIATOR. Very often the planning representative is the one who puts forward suggestions and new ideas. In part this is a natural result of the broad perspective such a staff needs to build, plus the necessary personal backgrounds. The role of initiator is a frequent one.

INSTRUCTOR. The planning function member has to help and to teach continually. The nature of the challenge will vary, from subtle guidance to a group of managers who do not know

163

how to put together a formal plan, to instruction of sophisticated groups who want information on new techniques, new market information sources, and so forth. Corollary to the Planning role in finding new information for the organization is the task of teaching the interested parties how to use it.

DOCUMENTOR. When a group has had a particularly productive discussion of its business strategy, or has made other significant decisions, someone should summarize the conclusions and circulate them, so the group will remember what they decided and can build from there the next time. Minimum effective formality is the rule — but when something comes by that really needs to be recorded, the planning staff member should either make the record, or make sure that the task is assigned to someone else who will carry it out.

ARCHITECT OF THE FUTURE. The management of any significant enterprise has the opportunity to shape its own environment — Drucker calls it 'creating the future' — by finding desirable viable patterns and bringing them into being. Successful programs have created new markets, new distribution systems, new technologies and new life styles. Corporate proposals have led to new regulations and controls over the business environment — whether tariff restrictions on competition or redefinition of limitations on product usage.

As the future is created, line management must be the builder because line power and authority are required. However, a planning representative has a very real opportunity to be the architect, by helping to find and define the potentials and bring them to management together with proposals for action.

PLANNER. Only rarely can the planning function member plan — only in those cases when he or she is directing work. Of course each of us plans for our own activities, as should the planning representative, but most of the other work is in helping others to plan, rather than planning.

The Contribution Of The Planning Function

The work of Planning can be summarized simply in three points: (I) as appropriate, to perform all of the above roles, plus anything else which will help the line management planning process to flow forward, and (II) to gather the information for planning as discussed in Chapter VIII, and (III) to keep well informed personally so as to be prepared to perform the first two components well.

In the process of information gathering, the gatherers learn. But not all of those associated with the planning function participate in all of the information gathering, particularly if the foresight role has been assigned to a part of the group. In any case each member of the planning function needs some contact with outside experts and with the information-gathering organizations that specialize in new outlook material for planning staffs, and some professional interchange with others who face the same challenges in other organizations.

These requirements are not difficult to meet, if the Planning budget allows for some time away from the job site for outside seminars and activities and funds for the necessary expenses. Several professional organizations provide a forum for professional interchange among managers and planning staff members on planning topics,[1] and a very large assortment of seminars and programs is available.

The work of the planning function has been defined as that of making the line planning process effective. Another way of stating the same thing is to consider the planning function as an expense intended to reduce the management time required for planning and increase the value of the plans which result. Any planning staff should be willing to be measured for its cost-effectiveness in maximizing the value of management planning.

FOOTNOTES

[1]The two largest organizations focusing on planning in the U.S. are the Planning Executives Institute, P. O. Box 70, Oxford, Ohio 45056 and the North American Society for Corporate Planning, 1406 Third National Bldg., Dayton, Ohio 45402. The Institute for Management Sciences (TIMS) has a College on Planning and there are regional planning groups. Other countries have their own planning societies also, such as the Society for Long Range Planning (UK).

CHAPTER XVIII

MATCHING PLANNING TO
ORGANIZATIONAL NEEDS

For the planning function to add value, and to help management to maximize the quality and timeliness of its decisions, the planning system must be adapted to the particular needs of the organization, as has been discussed in previous chapters. And, while every organization is to some degree individual and different so that every planning system should be different, between large and small organizations, productive and service organizations, public and private sector organizations, for-profit and not-for-profit organizations, there are differences in the appropriate type of planning effort and its emphasis. The purpose of this chapter is to identify and discuss some of these differences.

Differences Between Large And Small Organizations

When an executive of General Electric or some other large corporation describes an effective corporate planning system, members of the audience take notes and some attempt to set up that sort of system in their own corporations. A literal duplicate of one corporate planning system almost never works, because the internal culture, personality and decision pattern of different organizations differs so much — but often there are features that can be adapted.

However, the exciting presentations are often from very large organizations, such as GE, and managers or planning staff from smaller companies find difficulty in using the ideas. In the first place the necessary degree of formality of a planning system increases in proportion to the size of the organization. Someone has said that formality and paper volume increase as the square of annual sales. This may be an exaggeration, but the larger the company, the more need to have things carefully written down, the more staffs with need to review the proposals, and the more levels in the organization through which ideas and approvals must filter.

In adapting from small to larger organizations the systems and procedures tend to get more elaborate as the organization gets more complex. A small organization or a larger one with a simple structure and few geographic locations can handle planning with a minimum of formality, if that is the style of its management, and should not cumber the planning with more procedure than necessary. But as the number of business units and geographic centers increases, and as the nature of the organizational linkages becomes more complex, more must be carefully written in order that it be accurately communicated and correctly remembered in all of the areas.

The other major difference between large and small organizations is the differing availability of specialized staffs. A major multinational is likely to have special staff for every component of the information-gathering and planning process. In a small organization the managers each have several tasks and may depend on consultants and outside services for specialized information, or may do without it.

In a small organization, or a small unit of a large organization, the line managers have the same planning task as in a large organization, and less specialized help in doing it. This disadvantage is balanced by the ability to work much less formally, and, in most cases, to make decisions and take action much more rapidly. Many of the inherent advantages lie with the small organization, if the managers can separate themselves from the business sufficiently to establish a strategic overview when it is needed, and are creative enough to get the specialized information that they need for strategic overview planning.

In a large organization the line manager is better supported by staff and more cumbered by procedure, but has a larger pool of resources to draw on. The resource advantage is an important one, but frequently large organizations fail to get the advantage of it, because they lack a strategic overview, or because their decision processes get excessively elaborate and time-consuming.

Planning For Productive And For Service Processes[1]

One major distinction in planning processes is derived from the difference in function between various operating units. Some units have a productive purpose, and others provide a service.

The units with a productive purpose exist in order to make or process something. Both the need for the unit and the evaluation of its performance can be based on the quantity, quality and cost of the output.

Service units do not have this sort of output. They function in support of the productive efforts, so that the demand for their services is a derived demand. The evaluation of their output is also derived, from their contribution to the efficiency and effectiveness of the productive units.

Production, distribution and sales are productive functions, in each case with a tangible output of units produced, orders handled, or sales achieved. All three depend on the services of an effective personnel function, but personnel can measure only derived contributions to the whole. Even though employee turnover ratios and staff cost per employee hired or fired may be calculated, it can never be entirely clear how much the personnel function contributes to overall profits.

Maintenance has a similar service role. While many tasks are measured against engineered performance standards as an aid to maintenance management, the intangibles of the way that the service benefits the output from the productive units have much more to do with the real contribution of maintenance to the operating whole.

Other functions, such as research, are justified by their productive output, of new products in this case, even though the time lags may be long and the measurements difficult. But the planning function, like most other corporate staffs, is a service unit and has little tangible output. It can be measured only by estimating its contribution to making the total enterprise function effectively.

Whether each of the various components of an organization is primarily of a productive or a service nature will not necessarily be determined by its location in the organization. Inside of an administrative staff unit a printing and duplicating function may be operated as a productive unit subject to direct competition with outside vendors for best cost, delivery and quality. Yet the scheduling office in a major production unit may have no performance measures other than its service in providing workable schedules.

This comparison between productive and service functions is equally valid in organizations other than business enterprises. While most governmental organizations exist primarily to perform a particular public service, some of their components may be managed as productive units; e.g., the U.S. Government Printing Office.

The importance of the distinction between productive and service functions is in the fundamentally different psychology of the resulting management process. This is due to the nature of the performance measures, to which the managers respond[2], and therefore to the justification for the existence of the unit.

The productive processes are tested for effectiveness by the ability to generate a profit or a profit contribution. The service processes tested for efficiency by the ratio between the operating costs and the benefits perceived by the rest of the organization. The management tasks of the two types of units are almost exactly parallel. Both can draw from the same reservoir of management principles in planning, organizing, staffing, directing and controlling the processes aimed at achieving the organizational objectives. The difference is in the way that the management control process works, and by its working affects the behavior of the managers in charge of particular units.

A productive unit justifies not only its existence but any desired additional investments or increases in expenses primarily by its ability to produce more or to produce it for less. It can sometimes get resources it does not really need if the outputs are very favorable, and sometimes fails to fulfill even critical priorities when the bottom line looks bad. A service unit lacks any such direct justification, and must deal entirely with the management perception of the benefits from its services, as compared with their cost. Due to the intangible nature of the benefits, the process inevitably becomes somewhat subjective and political.

Since the planning process used by the management of an organizational unit is an integral component of its management process and geared to the achievement of its management goals, this means that the planning process of the two different types of units must be focused on achieving two fundamentally different types of management objectives. One is a bottom-line output measure and the other a politically acceptable cost/benefit ratio. Since productive and service units occur in various mixtures within different parts of most major organizations, the planning function needs a perception of the difference in planning requirements, both for those who must operate the two different types of units, and for their superiors who must maintain delegation and control over the two types of operations.

The planning process for an organization devoted primarily to rendering service will differ from that of an organization primarily devoted to productive efforts, because of the differing pattern by which the organization justifies its existence. The planning process of an organization focused on service must emphasize the benefit/cost ratio of these services, and promote as effectively as possible to keep the constituency supporting the services convinced that these benefits far exceed their cost. The judgment sought from this constituency is one of belief and perception, so that the arguments are generally framed on subjective grounds, and presented or lobbied in that way which will have the greatest impact on these beliefs.

By contrast, an organization whose primary purpose is productive has a bottom-line measure from which it is difficult to escape. Its planning process orients around the revenues which will be generated, the profits which will be received, and the best way to present and defend them. The two types of business organizations may have very similar management planning needs and may develop parallel planning systems, but they will be oriented and operated quite differently because of the different sorts of approval processes to which the two types of organizations are subject.

Differences Between Public And Private Sector Organizations

As follows from the above discussion, the difference between the planning processes in public and private sector organizations is keyed primarily to the differences in the approval processes. The tools and the planning needs of management are largely the same, but the world from which a public sector organization receives approval and funding may be radically different.

A public sector organization often builds incrementally on its past, using its existence as a justification for continuation of its services, and attempting to negotiate for funding only on the size of the budget increases necessary to continue and expand its function. This has been a very successful tactic, and although the zero-base budgeting concept was devised specifically to cancel out this approach to obtaining funds, politically adept managers will undoubtedly continue to expand their budgets from year to year in this way for the foreseeable future.

Another key tactic of many public sector organizations is that of building a constituency. This constituency is the group desiring or dependent on the service. The Veterans Administration has built a strong constituency and can draw automatic support for any challenge to its funding from a wide range of powerful organizations who have made themselves important in the re-election of members of Congress.

In the same way most other service-focused organizations have constituencies. The Army Engineers have long worked to develop relationships with key members of Congress, and to plan the necessary harbor, dredging and levee work so that it will benefit these supporters sufficiently so that they will in turn defend the engineers against challenges to their budgets or projects.

These are but two well-known examples of a pervasive process. Any welfare department or Department of Public Works has a constituency, as does the Tennessee Valley Authority or the Port of New York Authority. The underlying planning process is the same, but the focus is different due the need to cater to this constituency.

For-Profit And Not-For-Profit Organizations

The planning problem and process in a not-for-profit organization is not essentially different, in that the management needs are to be served by effective assistance in the planning. However, most not-for-profit units are service-focused, and also require the good will and support of an outside constituency for their continued existence.

Thus the efforts of the organization are divided between management of an effective operation, and catering to these key constituencies. Often not-for-profit groups have several types of constituencies for which to care.

A museum, for example, has need of the good will of the general public and often derives some of its revenue from the fees and purchases as they walk through. But it is more interested in converting the interested public into museum members, who have a closer relationship and pay more.

And beyond the many grades of personal and organizational members are the sponsors — those who can be persuaded to give funds. The sponsors vary from individuals and corporations who will donate, to various levels of government who can be persuaded to include the organization in current budgets, and to governmental and foundation groups who will approve grants for specific projects.

The management of any effective not-for-profit organization focuses heavily on the strategy for building and maintaining a strong, contributing constituency. Much of the current difficulty in the not-for-profit area has come because organizations once supported by individual philanthropists find that this can no longer be the basis for an organization that is viable over time — a broader constituency must be found, and many of today's not-for-profit organizations have not learned how to do this. The organizational planning process and its tools are essentially identical — it is the emphasis toward which the process is directed that is different.

Planning In Different Types Of Organizations

While there are differences between large and small organizations, productive and service organizations, private and public sector organizations, and profit or not-for-profit organizations which are useful in designing an appropriate planning process, these are differences in emphasis and justification. All of these types of organizations draw on the same underlying planning tools and techniques and require the similar skills for their management.

FOOTNOTES

[1]George C. Sawyer, "Why Society Needs Good Management," *Atlanta Economic Review,* September/October 1978, pp 25-27

[2]Peter Drucker, "Managers Respond To Their Performance Measures," lectures at New York University.

CHAPTER XIX

INNOVATION IN ORGANIZATIONS, AND THE PLANNING PROCESS

Planning — In Order To Have A Future

Planning is a means to anticipating and influencing the future. Day-by-day the future unfolds, but the role in that future for a particular organization is far from certain. Products and markets grow old, technologies and life styles change, and the momentum of past success runs out. To have an attractive future a business must plan for it, by considering the probable changes, defining the requirements for continued success in the future, and laying out a course of action likely to achieve that desired degree of success.

Many successful companies fail to move out beyond the base built by past success because management does not really believe that adversity could overtake existing products and markets, at least until some far future time, and because they have so circumscribed their perceptual horizons in order to concentrate on their present business and achieve success that the possibility of any radically new approach to familiar products and markets becomes incomprehensible.

The U.S. electronics industry failed to concede that consumer product applications for U.S. transistors were yet practical, until the Japanese developed the products and displaced the U.S. companies from the market. And firm after firm turned down the opportunity to develop the invention which became the Xerox copier.

These failures occur because the normal and correct point of view for routine operation of existing business happens also to be a point of view which assures almost total strategic blindness to the larger dimensions where the future of the business is determined. Too few managements seem to realize this, and continue to operate year after year unaware of their inability to see ahead.

The commitment to new areas, technologies and processes must be a conscious and considered act, if a firm is to move out beyond the boundaries of existing business in other than a random manner. Only if a strategic overview is established, validated and used as the basis for conscious strategy revision is that strategy likely to have any real prospects for viability and success. This detection, selection and development of corporate opportunity should be a conscious, managed part of the planning process. This also gives the planning function a role in aiding in conversion of a specific opportunity to a defined, communicated and implemented strategy.

Drucker defined an innovation as a useful new combination of resources, and planning deals continually with the best way that a given pool of resources can be used. It will, therefore, be in the forefront of the innovation process, if it performs effectively.

In its information-collecting role the planning staff gathers facts on all of the factors affecting the firm and its markets, and especially on new developments of all types. In its catalytic role as it assists line managers in the formulation of their plans, the planning function has the opportunity and the obligation to challenge the best minds available, to see what new solutions to urgent problems of the firm can be generated.

The planning process accomplishes little if innovations do not result, and if useful new combinations of the firm's resources are not devised to solve current operating and corporate strategy problems. Planning is a creative process, and the innovations which result are a measure of its success, and of whether the planning unit is effective in its catalysis of the innate creativity of the minds which share in the planning.

The corporate planning process and the corporate planning function logically become the center of the creative, innovative activity in the firm, as a consequence of the creative role of planning itself. This is not to overlook the role of research or other innovation-focused departments, except to note that their innovation role is focused and circumscribed by the role and the resources assigned to that specific department, where Planning has the generalist role.

As the logical center of the firm's innovative thinking, the planning function can build recognition for this role, and is often invited by various parts of the organization to lead in proposing to management a wide variety of new activities. If this leadership position is used wisely and well, it can tremendously enhance the actual and perceived value of the planning effort.

Planning As The Innovation Catalyst

In addition to its direct support of line management, an effective planning effort generates a continuing collection and redefinition of the problems and opportunities of the firm. This list of problems and opportunities is also a list of opportunities for innovation, so that a part of the internal effort of the planning function should be to review this list and choose areas where an effort should be started to generate the needed innovation.

At least three major types of innovation-triggering activity are possible: (I) analysis in preparation for an innovation-focused

174

management decision, (II) a search for missing information or expertise needed for the solution of a problem, and (III) creation of an innovation task force to generate new solutions to a significant problem.

An example of the first type of approach was a business which was not a designer or seller of equipment but found that the future of its new products hinged on the rate at which a major new piece of equipment would be introduced to the market. Alternatives included direct investment in its own development of such a product, even though this involved unfamiliar technologies and markets, investment in the development process of one of the firms already in this market, or acquisition of one of these firms. The default option was to hope that someone would develop and market the necessary equipment before the delay hurt the growth of the business seriously.

Here the planning unit aided line management in defining the innovation potential, first by pointing out the issue as timely for strategic decision. Then it carried out a study of the markets, issues and costs related to the various alternatives, as well as gathering opinions as to the probable results from existing industry development programs, and thus provided the basis for an informed decision.

An example of the second type of participation can be drawn from the evaluation of a new surgical product which appeared to have a large market potential, except for uncertainties about the raw materials, which were unfamiliar. Planning obtained outside expert opinion on these materials from several different sources, and based on this information management decided to proceed with development. The Planning contribution to the resulting innovation was the timely information on a critical issue which was impeding decision.

An example of the third type of innovation-triggering activity occurred after a planning representative aided a marketing group in defining the most desirable types of new products. As it became clear that the lack of these new products was a serious strategic weakness for that business, Planning at the request of the marketing group assembled a task force which undertook a structured creativity approach to the concepts necessary for the development of this family of products.

Structured creativity approaches to innovation have been successful because they stimulate new insights from the mind of those with the best knowledge of the markets and technology, by their interaction under careful guidance. In this case the project was managed internally because a member of the planning unit was skilled in this type of innovation leadership, and no outside market or technical knowledge resources appeared to be needed. The innovation task force was made up of employees from a variety of different technical and business disciplines, with a deliberate mixture of those with a high degree and a very low degree of knowledge of the details of the specific situation.

The successful result of the task force effort was a series of five technical concepts for the desired family of new products. Two were discarded after preliminary laboratory work, and one due to unfavorable costs, but the other two demonstrated their expected potential. A decision was made as to which concept would give the greater competitive advantage in the market place, and product development proceeded successfully.

Structured creativity techniques deserve wider application, and the planning unit is often in the best position to see the opportunity and turn it into action and success. Many projects benefit by drawing on technical expertise from outside of the firm however, and a more powerful approach to the innovation problem can often be constructed if a consultant firm specializing in structured creativity services assists the planning function, although in the instance cited above no assistance from outside resources was required.

The role of Planning in the three types of innovation opportunities cited above varies from that of the analyst in support of the management planning process, to catalyst of the organization's inherent creative processes, and to leader of specific efforts to find innovative solutions to organizational problems and opportunities, whether by a structured creativity approach or otherwise.

Planning Versus The Organization

One of the key roles of the planning function in contributing to the creativity of the organization should be in resisting the dead weight of organizational bureaucracy. Organization is necessary, and a degree of formality is necessary, but the inherent processes of organization and formalization are self-perpetuating and self-generating. They will rapidly choke off the vitality of any organization if management permits these processes to dominate.

In order for an organization to function, relationships and procedures must be defined. The normal human process is then continually to refine and improve the accuracy and detail of these definitions. The consequence is a growth of form and procedure depersonalizing the system, and at least symbolically substituting titles and job descriptions for people, so that they can become interchangeable within grades and categories. This standardization to facilitate the functioning of the organization is a very substantial levelling force, tending to restrain all out-of-procedure occurrences, including most types of creativity.

An organization's functional task delegation also becomes the basis for a project review process. When a given proposal to management goes out for critical analysis, each unit is expected to perform its review in a definitive way with regard to its assigned area of expertise. Most important innovations are born in pieces; that is, the initial insight is but a partial innovation[1] in one narrow dimension. Given the potential unlocked by that insight, the innovation needs to be completed in its other dimensions. Others extend that insight into other dimensions until a useful new combination of resources is achieved. For example, a new technical insight will often face initial issues as to appropriate means of production, marketing or finance, and all of these must be successfully addressed before the innovation is achieved.

But the organizational review processes tend to require that a proposal be circulated for review and funding approval as soon as it moves across the boundaries between specialties. Usually this occurs as soon as the first area has defined the potential in its own dimension but before extension into other dimensions has been attempted, because that requires approval and funding. But by the nature of the organizational relationships each functional review is required to point out the gaps in the proposal, and only the originating area is in a position to have a favorable report.

Most projects are found to be incomplete, and it is never organizationally safe for the reviewing staffs to minimize the obstacles. Therefore, the normal review process will produce an overwhelmingly negative appraisal of almost any partial innovation regardless of intrinsic merit, and few new ideas survive.

The management control aspects of organizational review processes are important in conserving assets and avoiding errors. But as a result any organization, by the inherent nature of its bureaucracy, has a heavy anti-creative bias.

Since an organization in its intrinsic nature is anti-creative, the only way that a large firm can achieve any creative or innovative step is for the top management to keep continual pressure in restraint of these organizational forces. As line authority, the top management voice is the essential one, but the planning staff has a role, because only that staff may know where the pressure is most needed.

The spontaneous organizational forces in any firm will choke off creative and innovative activity, including planning, if they are permitted by management to do so. The planning process must successfully resist these organizational forces in order to survive. This role also reinforces the position of the planning function as the logical locus of the creative and innovative activity of the firm. Planning success in this role requires (I) top management support, (II) an understanding of the innovation needs and potential of the firm both within and outside of normal planning activity, and (III) skill in articulating the processes which develop and realize this innovation potential.

A default of this role by the planning function is likely to mean that the firm's creative potential is not realized, except for those narrow innovation components assigned to research or other specific departments. As the locus of the innovative and creative activity of the firm, Planning can help to steer sound partial innovations to completion, can help to get critical gaps closed, and can often help to protect important new potentials from premature organizational judgment.

Planning And Innovation

Planning is a management process and an organizational process essential to the future of any firm, and effective in proportion to the quality of the planning effort and of the strategic overview from which the strategy is formulated.

The planning function is logically the key aid and catalyst to the line management planning process; this is the basic, work-horse role which justifies its existence. But by the nature of its activity, and by its need to be the center of resistance to the organizational forces which could otherwise choke both planning and the firm's vitality, planning also becomes the locus of the creative, innovative activity. While much of this role is a quiet extension of its information-clearinghouse and staff support activities, the planning function also has the opportunity to take initiative in defining and resolving some of the basic innovation problems and opportunities of the firm. This is an effective, visible role, and one of the few in which Planning can make a clear contribution apart from the management activities it normally assists.

FOOTNOTES

[1]George C. Sawyer, "Innovation In Organizations," *Long Range Planning,* December 1978, pp 53-57.

CHAPTER XX

PLANNING AS A CREATIVE PROCESS

Throughout this book a consistent attempt has been made to emphasize the potential contribution of planning to the welfare of a corporation or other business enterprise, and to emphasize that the same contribution potential exists in public sector, not-for-profit and any other goal-directed organizations. This planning contribution is of two types: (I) the contribution from the line managers who do the actual planning — and who by the quality of their planning, decisions and action make the organization succeed or fail, and (II) the contribution of planning staffs and others who help to increase the effectiveness of these managers, and thereby to increase the chance that the organization will prosper.

Management is a highly variable quantity in today's world. Many organizations have weak or marginally competent managers in some key positions. Others have individually good managers not integrated into an effective team, or a good management team afflicted with strategic blindness and not aware of the bad quality of its decisions.

No amount of planning can overcome the failures of bad management, especially because the active planning itself must be done by the same managers. But a good planning system — as measured against that organization's needs — and a competent planning function can create conditions under which a given group of managers can perform much better than otherwise. Strategic blindness becomes less possible. Open audit of strategies and actions makes weaknesses more apparent and correctible. The teamwork and discipline of an organized approach to plan creation and review helps each manager to function at a higher proportion of his or her ultimate potential.

The better and more effective organizations attempt to design a system so that competent managers can synergize with each other, build on each others strengths, and achieve major successes as a group. And a key part of this pattern for success is an appropriate, effective planning system supported by a capable, effective planning group.

A Plan As A Closed Analysis Of An Open System

A most critical element is the quality of the planning process — any given plan is but a snapshot of this process at a moment in time. However, decisions flow out of this process each in the context of a specific plan. That is, in the course of reaching a decision management frames a plan and makes the decision in that context. While a written document may or may not capture this plan, it exists at that moment as the basis of the decision.

So, while the quality of the planning process tends to set an upper limit on the quality of the strategy and of the resulting decisions, the quality of any specific decision tends to be limited to the quality of the plan in which it emerged. But a plan, as a snapshot of a process, is a closed analysis of an open system. The organization is an open system whose variations can be accommodated by the planning process, but any specific plan is a closed system, bounded by a specific series of premises about variables outside of the system.

Since the specific plan quality tends to set a limit on the quality of the decisions emerging through it, it follows that, among other things, the quality of a given management's decisions is controlled by the quality of the premises about the outside world upon which it builds its plans and decisions. Line management often must make decisions without the time for a full audit of the premises underlying them. Instead it draws on the current stock of premises upon which the planning processes is operating, and relies on the planning function to see that these premises are up to date. Planning keeps the entire spectrum of relevant premises under review, and as necessary brings critical premises to management for review together with adequate information for their reappraisal.

This process requires an effective planning function, so that information requirements are anticipated and issues brought up for decision in a timely manner. It also requires management decisions made from a strategic overview perspective and Planning audit of the effectiveness of this overview, so that management does not make decisions blindly and unaware of its strategic blindness.

Planning For The Management Needs Of An Industrial Society

The planning process, which is a part of management and best developed by good managers, is a key theme in today's society. The same trends which have taken firms beyond the old norms of the genius-entrepreneur have created an industrial society of great complexity and great interdependence between its parts. As complexity increases, the premium on and need for good planning also increases.

The modern industrial society is creating new problems as it grows, and these problems now include limitations on energy, pollution and growth. The U.S. industrial society has the highest standard of living in the world or in history, but its illnesses are still manifest. Over the years since the New Deal, the U.S. has devoted a larger and larger fraction of its resources to social programs, in an attempt to cure some of these social ills.

Today a substantial fraction of national resources is devoted to social programs including various forms of welfare, and to administrative and regulatory processes. Since the living standard of the country is determined primarily by the rate at which it manufactures the wealth that our living consumes, the rise in wealth production has clearly been rapid enough to fund social programs and to provide an increase in living standards.

With new limitations appearing in the industrial system and with the rising cost of social programs, national and corporate management will be under increasing pressure to increase the productivity of resources, and to deliver needed services at lower cost. The call will be for better management in both private and public sectors, which will require better planning as a key ingredient. The challenge to managers and to their planning support will be to achieve greater efficiency and effectiveness. This means getting more and better results from the actions laid out in advance and executed.

Planning As A Creative Process

In emphasizing the difficulties and challenges of a planning process, this book has returned again and again to the potential for aiding line management in directing its actions to more effective channels. This is the essence of the role of the planning function.

Planning itself is an essential activity, and the role of the planning function is essential to a successful planning process in a large organization. The purpose is to arrive at better decisions, and to lay out better actions as the firm moves into the future. The cost of planning activities, including the management time, can only be justified by considering the quality of the decisions which have resulted, and judging whether value has been added beyond the cost of the planning effort.

Value-added planning is the goal, and the basic activity must be well-performed to achieve this. However, this performance also brings Planning to a leadership in the firm's innovation processes. Carefully managed this leadership produces significant results, and represents one of the better ways of keeping management aware of how great the value added by the planning activity really is.

Planning can and should be a creative role. Managers and their staffs should insist on this creativity, first by stripping away the routine, the repetitive, the non-contributing formalism that tends to grow around any corporate process, and then by demanding the ingenuity, the innovation, the creativity that brings planning to the level of a major competitive advantage in building and protecting the future of the organization.

The challenge is to aid and catalyze new and effective approaches to business problems, based on new and useful combinations of the resources available to the business. This is innovation, by the dictionary and in practice. This is a creative process, where the potential for invention and contribution to the progress of the enterprise is greater than in almost any other corporate role.

FOOTNOTES

[1]George C. Sawyer, "Why Society Needs Good Management," *Atlanta Economic Review,* September/October 1978, pp 25-27.

GLOSSARY

CASH FLOW: A progress measure and control element, to predict and track the implementation pattern of a strategy and to gauge its nearness and vulnerability to sudden failure or success.

CONSULTING: A private advisory role in which the first allegiance, within reasonable boundaries of discretion, is to the client, where normal staff activities have primary allegiance to their organizational superior.

FOCUS: The defined relationship with the customers and the market place upon which a strategy is based.

GOALS: Those achievements towards which management wants the organization to strive as it seeks to fulfill its mission.

LEVERAGES: The specific incentives to buy a given product or service, as perceived by the buyer; the reasons why the customer sees the deliverable product or service as a pacifier for specific needs.

MANAGEMENT OPERATING SYSTEM: The system of linkages between different components of the operation by which the different departments and operating units communicate with each other, and by which management directs the operation and receives information on its performance.

MISSION: A statement of the role in which a business — or other organization — hopes and plans to serve society. Thus, the mission is the franchise in the market place on which a business is based — and the hunting license making legitimate its pursuit of profit.

PLANNER: One who has the authority and responsibility necessary to lay action out in advance and implement it.

PLANNING: An analytical process which encompasses an assessment of the future, the determination of desired objectives in the context of that future, the development of alternative courses of action to achieve such objectives, and the selection of a course (or courses) of action from among such objectives.

— Scott[2]

183

PLANNING: Action laid out in advance.

— Sawyer

POSITION: Any consequence of past operations which can become a resource aiding in the design and implementation of new strategies. Valuable positions include those based on brand names and other market success, raw material costs or control, superior or protected processes and technology, cost advantages, and firm ties to customer need and habit patterns.

RESOURCES: The necessary combination of technology, equipment, time, talent, and position required to implement a strategy successfully.

STAFFS supply information, advice, and various other types of service and support to LINE managers, who are those charged with responsibility for the functions necessary for the day-to-day performance of the economic role on which the enterprise is based.

STRATEGIC BLINDNESS: Insufficient perspective of the total flow of events to deal successfully with formulation of corporate strategy.

STRATEGIC OVERVIEW MANAGEMENT: Management acting from a perspective above the level of routine operating considerations, which accepts and evaluates information normally rejected by the information barriers of the individual managers and of the organization, and which discovers and acts on patterns relevant to present or future strategic needs or plans. This requires an effective concentration on corporate operations, the management of corporate social impact, of opportunity, of course correction, and on self-renewal processes, so that day-by-day energy can be focused on those areas most strategic to the continued existence and continued success of the firm.

STRATEGY: A road map to the goals; that is, an assembly of the elements which, when linked together effectively, permit a plan which moves the business forward towards the specific accomplishments it has chosen to attempt.

PRODUCT STRATEGY deals with achieving goals related to successful conception, development, production and marketing of specific goods or services.

184

BUSINESS STRATEGY deals with achieving a mission and goals related to the successful management of a business unit.

RESOURCE STRATEGY deals with allocation of the available resources between business units or other alternative uses.

INDEX

A

ABI-Inform, 105
Advocate role of planning function, 160
Aluminum cans, 65
American Hospital Supply, 49
Analyst role of planning function, 162
Appalachia, 72
ARA Services, 25-8
Architect of the future role of planning function, 164
Arthur D. Little, 79, 104, 119
Available product family, 118, 120-1
Available products, 117-118, 120-1
Avon, 27, 39

B

Beer, Stafford, 56
Bell (AT&T), 84
Bell Laboratories, 151
Boston Consulting Group, 79
Brown, Arnold, 106

C

Carnegie, Andrew, 117
Cash flow, 42-4, 183
Center for Futures Research, 105
Chase Econometrics, 104
Chevrolet, 27-8, 40-1
Chrysler, 68
Clean Waters Act, 98
Club of Rome, 98
Coal mine safety, 72
College on Planning (TIMS), 165
Commodities, 115, 117, 120-1, 128, 130, 132

Communicator role of planning function, 159
Competitive action potential, viii, 122-123, 131
Computer support, 153-4
  -aggregation, 153-4
  -simulation, 153-4
Concentration barriers, 54-56, 57, 90, 132
Conscience role of planning function, 162
Consolidated Edison, 27-8
Constituency requirement, 169-171
Consulting, 4, 183
Consultant role of planning function, 158
Cookbook planning, 30, 35
Corporate culture, 147, 150
Corporate social impact, viii, 57-8, 61-73
Counsellor role of planning function, 161
Craftsmanship, 119, 120-1

D

Data Resources, 104
Decision process, 2
Deliverable, 38, 42-4, 47
Diagnostician role of planning function, 162
Director role of planning function, 162
Display, 41-5
Documentor role of planning function, 164
Dow Chemical, 84
Drucker, Peter F., ii, 23, 146, 164, 174

E

Edison, Thomas A., 37
Einstein, 112
Entreprenuer role of planning function, 163
Environmental scanning, 106-7
Equal Employment Opportunity, 93-4, 103
Evaluator role of planning function, 162
Excessive formality, 155-6, 167
Exxon, 26

F

FDA, 83, 86
Facilitator role of planning function, 159
Find/SVP, 105
Fluorocarbon discharge, 65
Focus, 38-9, 40, 42-5, 115-124, 128-9, 131, 183
Ford, Henry, 40-1, 118
Foresight function, 85-7, 105-8, 110-114
Forrester, Jay, 98
Franchise, vii, 14, 20, 22, 24-8, 48-9
Frankenstein, 56
Function of operating units
-productive function, 167-170
-service function, 167-171
The Futures Group, 105

G-H

General Electric, 26, 66, 79-80, 143, 166
General Foods, 26-7, 47
General Mills, 59, 83
General Motors, 27-8, 40-1, 146
Generic drugs, 49
Genius-entrepreneur, 5

Goals, vii, viii, 1, 10, 13-14, 18, 19, 28, 29-36, 37, 50, 52, 128, 129, 133, 141, 145-6, 183
Goal tradeoffs, 29, 32, 34-5
Goldenberg, David I., 143
Harris, John S., 132
Herman's World of Sporting Goods, 25-6
Hoffman-La Roche, 117
Hooker Chemical, 67

I-J-K

Indiana Coal Association, 102-3
Initiator role of planning function, 163, 174-8
Innovation, ix, 46-50, 71, 77, 112, 163, 173-8
Innovator role of planning function, 163
Institute of Life Insurance, 106
Instructor role of planning function, 163
Integrator role of planning function, 159
Invisible hand, 72
Iran, 85, 87
ITT, 26
Jello, 26, 48
Kennedy, Senator Ted, 86
Koontz, Harold, 5
Krazy Glue, 119
Kuhn, Thomas, 97

L

LANCET, 86
Leader role of planning function, 162
Leavitt, Theodore, 121
Levels of focus, viii, 115-124, 128-9

188

190